Everyone knows that education is important – we are confronted daily by discussion of it in the media and by politicians – but how much do we really know about education? *Education: The Basics* is a lively and engaging introduction to education as an academic subject, taking into account both theory and practice. Covering the schooling system, the nature of knowledge and methods of teaching, this book analyses the viewpoints of both teachers and pupils. Key questions are answered, including:

- What is education and what is it for?
- Where does education take place?
- How do we learn?
- Who are the students?
- What is being taught in schools and universities and why?
- What is the state of education across the world?

With further reading throughout, *Education: The Basics* is essential for all those embarking on undergraduate courses in Education and Education Studies, and for those with an involvement in teaching at all levels.

Kay Wood recently retired as Head of the Department of Education and Childhood Studies at Bath Spa University. She has experience of secondary teaching and in-school training, and for twelve years acted as Access tutor, promoting wider access to education at all levels. Her primary research interests are international education, the sociology of education and education policy.

THE BASICS

EDUCATION

THE BASICS

kay wood

Routledge
Taylor & Francis Group

LONDON AND NEW YORK

First published 2011
by Routledge
2 Park Square, Milton Park, Abingdon, Oxon OX14 4RN

Simultaneously published in the USA and Canada
by Routledge
711 Third Avenue, New York, NY 10017

Routledge is an imprint of the Taylor & Francis Group, an informa business

© 2011 Kay Wood

British Library Cataloguing in Publication Data
A catalogue record for this book is available from the British Library

Library of Congress Cataloging in Publication Data
Wood, Kay, 1945-
  Education : the basics / Kay Wood.
    p. cm. – (The basics)
  Includes bibliographical references.
  1. Education. 2. Education–Philosophy. I. Title.
  LB14.7.W66 2011
  370–dc22
        2011000314

ISBN: 978-0-415-58954-3 (hbk)
ISBN: 978-0-415-58955-0 (pbk)
ISBN: 978-0-203-80918-1 (ebk)

Typeset in Bembo and Scala Sans
by Taylor & Francis Books

Printed and bound in Great Britain by
TJ International Ltd, Padstow, Cornwall

For Graham, with thanks

CONTENTS

ACKNOWLEDGEMENTS

I would like to thank Steve Ward, who worked tirelessly in editing my writing, often at very short notice, and to Graham Jones, who also contributed to the editing and provided support throughout the enterprise. The writing was greatly assisted by interesting conversations I had with my colleagues, in particular Andy Bord, Dave Hicks and Mike McBeth. Above all I am grateful to all those students over the years who have actively engaged with the issues and contributed to my own education.

LIST OF ABBREVIATIONS

CSE	Certificate of Secondary Education
DCSF	Department for Children, Schools and Families
DFES	Department for Education and Skills
EYFS	Early Years Foundation Stage
FE	Further Education
GCE	General Certificate of Education
GCSE	General Certificate of Secondary Education
HE	Higher Education
HEFC	Higher Education Funding Council
HLTA	Higher Level Teaching Assistants
IMF	International Monetary Fund
IQ	Intelligence quotient
LMS	Local Management of Schools
OECD	Organisation for Economic Co-operation and Development
Ofsted	Office for Standards in Education
PGCE	Postgraduate Certificate in Education
PISA	Programme for International Student Assessment
QAA	Quality Assurance Agency

QCDA	Qualifications and Curriculum Development Agency
SATS	Standard Assessment Tests
TA	Teaching assistant
TGAT	Task Group on Assessment and Testing
UNICEF	United Nations Children's Fund

INTRODUCTION

Welcome to this introduction to the study of Education. Unlike other subjects that may require work and effort to understand, people tend to think they know what education is. It is a familiar topic: a word in daily use. It's all around us. We go to college or university to get educated. We entrust our children to schools in the belief that they will become knowledgeable and skilled. Politicians of all persuasions continually tell us how important education is for the economy. We are bombarded with messages from the media. It is impossible to open a newspaper or listen to the television news without hearing something about education, often derogatory. Schools are failing, budgets have been slashed, children are not learning … On the bus, in the pub and at the hairdresser's people are expressing opinions. We may not know much about nuclear physics, but we are all experts on education.

But how much do we really know? How objective is our understanding? We may have personal experience of education, but does that equip us to make judgements about the education system as a whole? There is a deluge of information, but how do we assess its veracity? Much of what we read in the newspapers has been selected and interpreted by other people. The academic study of education helps with this. It gives us the ability to seek out facts, ask the right kinds of questions and examine the research that might provide answers.

EDUCATION AS SCHOOLING

In current thinking education is strongly linked with schooling. Typing the word education into a search engine immediately produces a wealth of information on schools and the government bodies responsible for them. The link between education and schooling is obvious. Pupils and students attend schools, colleges and universities and such institutions are part of the taken-for-granted fabric of our lives; but what exactly is their purpose and do we really need them in their present form? We assume schooling to be necessary and useful; but are we right to do so? Different countries have different approaches to schooling. English early-years education tends to be fairly formal with carefully documented targets for learning, but early-years education in Norway for example is less formal and more dependent on pupils' direct experience of the natural environment. In questioning the nature of schooling we need to suspend any belief we might have that the system we have personally experienced is better than, or even as good as, others.

There is a long history of educators who have been critical of state education. From Emile Rousseau to Rudolph Steiner and A. S. Neill there have been indictments of formal education and moves made to set up alternative schools. A lot of education has always taken place outside formal institutions. Some parents chose to educate their children at home and, particularly at primary level, the number of children educated outside school is increasing. We need to ask why so many people have been critical of formal schooling and what can be learnt from such criticisms?

EDUCATION AS THE ACQUISITION OF KNOWLEDGE AND SKILLS

A dictionary definition of education suggests that education is the process of acquiring or imparting knowledge and skills. There has been some discussion in British schooling of what this knowledge and these skills should be, but any discussion is curtailed because of a lack of discussion and agreement about the aims and purposes of education. The curriculum in schools has in many respects remained virtually unchanged since formal education began. Could it be that it is now out of touch with the world we are in, and if so what can be done to remedy the situation?

In describing education as the acquisition of knowledge and skills, dictionary definitions include the development of the ability to reason and think critically. This is vital in a world which has frequently used education to promote totalitarianism and where schools and teachers have become easy targets for bigots and despots. In the UK people tend to think they are secure from such threats, but democracy is fragile and demands constant vigilance, no less in our schools and universities than in the political arena.

EDUCATION AS THE PROCESS OF LEARNING

However we define education, whether in formal or informal settings, it is ultimately strongly related to the concept of learning. What can a study of learning teach us about what should happen in education? There have been huge advances in recent years in the under-standing of what learning is and how it can best be facilitated. From the progressive theorists to the constructivist psychologists and the recent understanding of how the brain functions the message is clear. Everyone learns best when they can connect what they are being presented with to what they already know. Whether teaching small children, adolescents or university students, it is necessary to start where the students currently are. Learning needs to be active and related to questions the learners themselves generate. How are education and learning connected? Is schooling in the forms it takes at present, the best way to promote learning?

EDUCATION AND THE MORAL DIMENSION

Education is not just the acquisition of knowledge and skills. There is also a moral dimension. Pupils need to know not only facts and figures, but how to evaluate their significance. There has to be informed debate around received knowledge. Albert Speer, a leading Nazi in World War II, was responsible for arms production in the Third Reich. He authorised the use of slave labour and conditions of production which led to the death of a very large number of people. He confessed to his involvement and was later imprisoned for his crimes. In later years he reflected on the consequences of having had the 'best' education possible at that time. He was a master of facts and the manipulation of data but what his education lacked, he claimed, was any moral sense. When he approved the statistics for moving workers around he was doing just that, accepting the figures. At no point did he connect the figures to real people or the dreadful situations he was forcing them into. Education cannot be neutral; it has to know the difference between right and wrong and offer a spirited defence of the former. The study of education involves the study of values. There are no easy answers in relation to this but we need to understand not only what our personal value positions are, but also the values that underpin different education systems. Only then can we make a reasoned critique of what is going on.

EDUCATION AS A POTENTIAL THREAT

David Orr writing in *Earth in Mind* points out that most of the problems we currently face, are a result of the actions of the most educated. The unschooled do not pose a threat to survival. Globally it is the educated who consume the most and waste the most. It is the educated bankers and economists who have contributed to the world recession. It is the educated who invest in policies which are ruining the world. They are not doing this necessarily with forethought, but are themselves the result of an education system which has often alienated students from the natural world and produced people whose main aim in life is to get wealthy. Worst of all it has produced an educated elite which is mostly unaware of its own ignorance.

David Orr asks us to consider whether our current education system, geared towards production and economic growth, is the right kind of education for the next generation who will have to grapple with the problems of climate change, population growth and energy issues which threaten our very survival.

WHAT DOES IT MEAN TO BE AN EDUCATED PERSON?

What does it then mean to be an educated person? We may have been well schooled, even have a university degree, but does that make us educated? People frequently say that what they most value they learned, on the job, at evening classes, or in conversations with others. In the recent film, *An Education*, an adaptation of Lynn Barber's account of her own adolescent experiences, the heroine rejects schooling in favour of a different kind of education, one that involves her seduction by a much older man. She later returns to school, a sadder and wiser student but one who feels she has definitely received an education.

Perhaps 'real' education is the province of the rich and clever of this world. Perhaps going to an expensive public school or a prestigious university makes you better educated. It may give you the knowledge, the vocabulary and the confidence to hold your own in public and professional discourse, but does this constitute a good education? It undoubtedly opens doors and affords access to positions of power, but is this enough? Does a good education involve the acquisition of something more than just power and prestige? Is the hallmark of a good education that it leads to self-knowledge and wisdom? Does education involve not just knowledge acquisition but also a sense of moral judgement and an understanding of what constitutes the good life?

EDUCATION AS AN ACADEMIC SUBJECT

Besides being a process, Education is also an academic subject in its own right. Students at university study it in the same way they learn other subjects such as English or Sociology. It has evolved as a branch of learning which is taught to undergraduate students and informs teacher training courses. In this capacity it draws on key concepts and theories from other disciplines such as sociology and psychology to illuminate and explain behaviour. It is much more than a theoretical subject, however. It is also about the practice and application of teaching and learning. Education raises questions, looks for answers and suggests solutions.

OUTLINE OF THE BOOK

This book is called *Education: the basics*. It is not intended, however, to be a simplistic guide to the subject. To understand anything we need to get to the heart of the matter, and education is no exception. This is an attempt to distil the evidence, basic facts, figures and theories which make up education and to present them in a form which is accessible. There is a temptation in studying education to take things for granted, to accept traditional explanations and not to question things too much. This book asks you to suspend belief and to question everything. The process may be difficult and uncomfortable on occasions since it brings us up against our own cherished beliefs and values. In addition, in order to understand what is happening in education today, we have to see how our educational system is grounded in the society in which we live. For this we need some understanding of politics and economics. Many people shy away from such topics, but to avoid them is to accept explanations which are not grounded in reality. Moreover this side of the story adds excitement and spice which an apolitical consideration of the subject would lack.

Chapter 1 begins with a history of state education in the UK in the past 140 years. Who has had access to education? How has schooling been organised and who has provided it? In order to be able to answer these questions it is necessary to understand the role the state has played and the philosophies of the political parties which have controlled it.

Chapter 2 asks: what are the purposes of education? It is impossible to judge whether an education system is successful unless there is a yardstick against which to measure it. The aims of education are varied and potentially conflicting. Which should be the most important and for what reasons?

Chapter 3 invites you to meet the pupils. Who is being educated in the UK at the current time? Which groups are doing well and which not so well? What are the reasons for this and what have the governments of the day being doing to improve things? What are pupils' views on their schooling?

Chapter 4 focuses on what we are teaching students in schools and universities. What is in the curriculum? Are we teaching pupils the right kind of knowledge and skills? Should we all be taught the same things and, if so, who should decide what these should be? Is there a danger of propaganda?

Chapter 5 looks at teaching, learning and assessment. How do these three elements interact in schooling? Do we have a theory of teaching and does it hold water? Do we know how pupils learn and are we providing the best environment for this to happen? Are we testing children too much?

Chapter 6 turns to the critics of state schooling. These range from the progressive educators of past times to de-schoolers and current critics from within the school system. Have we got schooling wrong? Are we ignoring the needs and voice of the pupils? Does education need a revolution in thinking?

Chapter 7 takes education beyond the confines of the UK. It looks at the state of the world and calls for an education that informs us not only of the facts but also of the reasons for current difficulties. It highlights the necessity for a change of direction and for all of us to become educated and involved.

WHY STUDY EDUCATION?

There are obvious reasons for studying education: the first being that it is an excellent preparation for teaching. Students learn amongst other things what the aims of the education system are, how they are delivered and what effect they have on pupils. But studying education is not just of interest to potential teachers. There are many other opportunities to work with children and young people in a variety of situations involving play schemes, health, criminal justice or family support. Understanding educational theory is crucial to undertaking such vocations. Education graduates also go on to work abroad for private, state or voluntary organisations as teachers or volunteers. Studying comparative education points the way to wider possibilities.

There are important instrumental motives for studying education, but beyond this there is now an urgent need for all of us to understand and debate the future of education and schooling. We live in a world under threat from climate change, dwindling resources and serious conflicts. Education has the potential to help us find answers, but it has to be an education which asks the right questions, faces current dilemmas head-on and empowers both us and our children to make necessary changes to our life styles. There has been a growing tendency in the UK in recent years for education to be in the hands of politicians and civil servants. Many ordinary people remain comparatively ignorant about how education operates and the degree to which it offers solutions to current difficulties. The time for ignorance has passed. The onus is on us all to understand the problems and get educated.

A FINAL NOTE OF CAUTION

This book has been written with every attempt being made to check the data and to verify that the points made are valid. The world changes very rapidly however and what was correct at the end of 2010 may not be so by the time the book is read. Moreover all books contain value judgements. As a reader you need to be constantly on your guard. Is the position the writer takes justified? Is there sufficient evidence? Even if the evidence is acceptable is the conclusion the one you would reach?

Far from being straightforward, education is a mysterious process. It is frightening and at the same time exciting. It defies definition. Learning continues throughout life. Education never ends. In this sense it is open to all of us, no matter who we are or what age we are. This is a beginning only. The rest is up to you. Enjoy the journey.

EDUCATION AND SCHOOLING

Most people link the idea of education with that of schooling. Pupils go to school and are taught a set curriculum. They take examinations and formal tests and leave school with or without certificates. They have received an education. This is a perception of school which many people can relate to and is thought to be what 'normally' happens in most Western societies. The definition itself suggests that education is largely a methodical approach to a body of knowledge agreed by relevant experts and then delivered to willing and unwilling learners alike. The definition becomes recognisable as what goes on in schools in the UK on a daily basis. Both state and private schools employ a curriculum, taught in stages to pupils of similar ages and with similar abilities. On closer scrutiny, however, this easy-to-understand description of schooling does not apply everywhere. Scandinavian countries, Norway Sweden, Finland and Denmark, for example have a different view of education from that of the rest of Europe. They organise schools and curricula in different ways, have different methods of teaching and put less stress on tests and examinations.

FORMAL EDUCATION IN THE UK

More than 90 per cent of children in the UK attend state-run primary or secondary schools.[1] The remainder go to privately controlled schools which range from elite public schools to evangelical Christian and Muslim schools as well as those professing an alternative approach to education, such as Steiner or Montessori schools. A growing number of children are home-educated. Education is compulsory for all from the age of five, but large numbers of children are now in pre-school settings: nursery, play school or similar establishment. For the majority, schooling begins at age three in pre-school, is continued in primary school up to the age of eleven and continues in secondary school until the official school-leaving age of sixteen.

Post-sixteen education is termed 'further education' (FE) and increasing numbers of pupils are staying on until age eighteen, some of them helped by government grants although the future of these is currently in question. Education for this age group may happen in schools which have sixth forms, or it may be pursued in colleges of further education. FE institutions teach General Certificate of Secondary Education (GCSE) courses but they also offer a range of other courses including work-based learning and community-based activities. Establishments which offer degree-level qualifications are termed institutions of 'higher education' (HE) and these include universities and some colleges. In recent times there has been a blurring of the boundaries between all these institutions so that it is now possible to study for degrees in colleges of further education. The creation of the new 14–19 curriculum in England and Wales with the amalgamation of academic and vocational skills has also changed the rigid division between secondary and further education.

The one thing that can be said with certainty is that there is little uniformity within the UK education system. Since political devolution in the late 1990s, things which apply in England may not apply in Wales. Scotland and Northern Ireland too have different systems. Within England itself there are diverse arrangements: most children attend primary and then secondary schools, but some parts of the country have a system of first, middle and upper secondary schools.

STATE SCHOOLS

Most schools in the UK are state-funded and parents do not pay fees. The money to run schools comes from taxes, but not all schools are funded in the same way and it is difficult to speak of a universal system. The majority of schools receive money from their local authority which comes from direct government grants and council taxes collected from all householders. The local authority decides how the funds are allocated to schools, but governors and head teachers have considerable power to decide how the money is spent. Local authorities remain responsible for the maintenance of school buildings and for ensuring adequate school places for all potential pupils.

In Wales and Scotland practically all schools are funded by their local authority, but in England an increasing number of schools answer directly to the Secretary of State for Education or to businesses and private donors. Academies are a recent development – state-run schools which receive a general annual grant from the Secretary of State for Education. A similar system is likely to apply to the recently instituted 'free schools' which are discussed more fully in Chapter 6. The questions about school funding are not just a matter of how much money each school gets: it is also important to consider who provides and controls the finance as they are likely to have considerable influence over how schools are run and what is taught in them.

PRIVATE SCHOOLS

The sons of the wealthy have been schooled from the earliest times. The private school, Harrow, for example, began admitting pupils for the first time in the sixteenth century. In the nineteenth century the growth of middle class wealth led to the rapid expansion of private schooling for boys. Many of England's notable public schools together with a large number of independent fee-paying schools were set up at this time. As the twentieth century progressed private education was extended to cater for girls. In addition a small number of other private schools offer a specific religious education. There are, for example, 126 full-time Muslim schools in England, the vast majority of which are privately financed. Catholic and Anglican schools, in contrast, are mostly state-funded. Private schools overall cater for about 7 per cent of the pupil population.[2]

STATE EDUCATION IN THE UK

Most people when they think about schools get an immediate picture of buildings – maybe old, maybe new – gates and fences, a flashing belisha beacon, perhaps with the lollipop lady, and the surrounding roads clogged up with traffic in the morning and mid afternoon. In any neighbourhood one is not far from a school and much of community life revolves around it. They are important land-marks, but also taken-for-granted institutions that we have come to believe have always been there and are now permanent features of modern life. It is easy to forget that schools are relatively new and have only existed in their current form for the last 140 years. The world seemed to have progressed satisfactorily without them for thousands of years prior to this; why was it necessary to institute them? In order to answer this question it is essential to understand a little of our history and the kind of state and economic system we live in.

The history of educational developments in England and Wales in the twentieth century is very much the history of state schooling. It is the story of the creation of a formal system of primary, secondary and further education and of the expansion of universities and other forms of higher education. Successive governments have decided who should have access to schooling, how it should be organised, where it should take place and even what should be taught and how. The Scottish education system from the beginning has been separate from that of England and Wales, but has largely ploughed a similar furrow. Summarising the history of education over 140 years is not easy, but it possible to identify four key phases in the development of state education in England and Wales. These are summarised in Table 1.

A quick glance at the table suggests that the story has been straightforward and followed a predictable trajectory. More and more children have gained access to education and stayed for longer and longer lengths of time in school. As increasing amounts of money have been spent on education, successive governments have intervened in the educational process to ensure that taxpayers' money is wisely spent. It all seems logical, self-evident and beyond dispute in the twenty-first century, but looked at in a little more depth this summary is simplistic. The path has not been clear-cut. Many of the reforms have been fought over and people have had widely divergent views as to what education is for and what form it should take. In order to understand some of these differences it is necessary to look at what part the state plays in education and how

Table 1 Four key phases in the development of state education in England and Wales

Date	Changes made	Outcome
1870 Education Act	*National system of elementary education.* Compulsory primary education for all children aged five to thirteen (extended to fourteen in 1918)	Majority stayed in primary school, secondary schools for wealthier only
1944 Education Act	*Secondary education for all.* Compulsory secondary education up to age of fifteen (extended to sixteen in 1972)	Tripartite system established. Children took eleven-plus test and were allocated to 'appropriate' secondary school
1970s onwards	*Comprehensive education.* Removal of the tripartite system. In most areas children went to their local secondary school	Far more pupils gained certification, but comprehensive schools criticised from a variety of perspectives
1988 Education Act	Control of schooling moved from local government to central government. Introduction of the local management of schools (LMS)	National Curriculum and testing introduced together with tighter inspection regime. Parental choice of schools

political philosophies have affected everything from the organisation of schools to the content of the curriculum.

GETTING EDUCATED ABOUT EDUCATION

Any mention of politics frequently produces a negative effect in students. 'I am here to learn about education' or 'I only want to find out how to teach children to read' are frequent statements. 'If I wanted to know about politics I would have taken a different course, read another book.' But this is to miss the point. Everyday life in classrooms is fundamentally affected by political beliefs and actions. The things teachers do in schools on a daily basis are informed by political opinion. Even such a seemingly innocent activity as the teaching of reading is subject to political influence, with politicians recommending, and sometimes seeking to enforce, the 'correct' way to do it. It is only by understanding and questioning these beliefs that we can come to a decision as to what we think the best course of action is. Digging below the surface is essential. Moreover, the story behind the table above and the events which accompanied it is interesting, exciting and fraught with controversy. To begin at the beginning we need to understand a little about the nature of the state we live in and the political philosophies which underpin it.

WHAT IS THE STATE?

The key factor in the development of education in the UK in the last 100 or so years has been the role that the state has played; but what exactly is the state and why does it play such a decisive part in all our lives? The state is everywhere; it regulates the conditions of our lives from birth to death. It is very difficult to define, and yet most of us have a sense of its power. It is essentially a group of institutions which together constitute the legitimate authority of any given country. The institutions consist of the government which passes the laws, the civil service which both advises the government and puts its policies in to practice and the judiciary which sees that the laws are enforced. The relationships between the various elements of the state are complicated, but in England it is undoubtedly the government of the day which has the most power. The state is, therefore, never neutral: it represents the views and ideological perspectives of the political party in power.

In the UK, national governments have a strong effect on education. The decisions they make reflect their own political convictions but also beliefs which are current in the country at the time. Looked at simply, there have been two key philosophical ideas which have underpinned British politics for the past 300 years: the first is 'liberalism' which recently has developed a new form called neo-liberalism and the second is 'social democracy'. It is helpful to understand the difference between these two philosophies because they throw light on what has happened in twentieth century education.

LIBERALISM

Liberalism has been an important philosophy which has had a strong effect on politics in both the UK and the United States. At one time or another, its beliefs have informed all political parties in Britain. Even more than this, over the years it has become a key ingredient in the way Britain views itself. Central to its philosophy is a strong belief in the rights of the individual which must be protected. Individuals must be free to make money and earn their livings as far as possible without interference from the state. The corollary of this is that the individual must take personal responsibility for his or her own actions. This tradition has favoured the individual over the state and has tended to see the state as only playing a minimal role in national life, a necessary evil.

A belief in individualism has also brought with it tolerance of hierarchy. There has been a tendency to accept that in any society where the individual is paramount there will inevitably be inequalities in wealth and income. These are considered justifiable because the onus rests on the individual to improve his or her lot in life; life is seen as a ladder all must climb. Some have naturally more talent than others and some put in more effort. This is the way of the world. In education policy it has contributed to a belief in elitism and to separate schools for children of different abilities. It has meant that the pursuit of equality has not been at the top of its agenda and this has fundamentally affected the kind of education system the UK has developed.

SOCIALISM AND SOCIAL DEMOCRACY

Socialism arrived at the end of the nineteenth century to challenge liberal ideas. It appeared in many different forms but in all cases there was a belief that the individualism of liberalism was unjust. Some socialists recognised the importance of the individual, but not at the expense of the wider community. Individual actions could not be sanctioned if they harmed others or led to the suffering of society as a whole. In the nineteenth century the unfettered power of capitalism had produced extremes of freedom and wealth for some and unbearable misery and enslavement for the rest. Socialists thought it was necessary to have strong state intervention to protect the weak.

In Western European countries socialist beliefs were transformed into social democracy. The capitalist system of production was accepted, but the avowed aim of social democrats was to transform capitalism into a more ethical enterprise where the needs of the many rather than the few are fully catered for. The state would be instrumental in achieving this transformation. The state is thus not the enemy, but rather the defender, of the public good. It has a duty to see that all citizens can participate in the social and economic life of the nation. People in positions of power must accept that they have responsibilities to others.

In the Scandinavian countries, Norway, Sweden, Finland and Denmark, these beliefs have infused society since World War II and prevailed whichever political party has been in power. They have produced systems of education which are strongly rooted in equality of opportunity for all. In the UK for a brief period post-1945 social democracy took hold and informed educational policy, but this way of thinking has not to date been a strong part of the way British people see themselves and Britain appears to remain largely in the liberal tradition.

This then is the background against which decisions about education have been taken. With these things in mind it is now appropriate to consider the four phases of state schooling in the UK to date and the key issues which have informed the kind of schooling we now have.

FOUR KEY PHASES IN THE DEVELOPMENT OF STATE EDUCATION IN ENGLAND AND WALES

ELEMENTARY EDUCATION FOR ALL: THE 1870 EDUCATION ACT

The first landmark moment in formal education in England and Wales was Forster's 1870 Education Act. It made elementary education compulsory for all children. Of course, schools existed prior to1870 but they tended to be very much on an *ad hoc* basis: private schools for the wealthy, schools run by voluntary organisations many of which were religious bodies, and endowed schools set up with money left by people when they died. The 1870 Act made for a sea change in education by setting up school boards which could for the first time enforce attendance. The new board schools filled the gaps left by the existing church schools and became the basis of a system which has remained complex up to and including current times.

Widespread education was late in coming to England and Wales. Scotland had a strong tradition of education which was well established in the eighteenth century and by the nineteenth century a good proportion of Scotland's population was already literate. By 1870 many European countries had set up national education schemes. England, however, in keeping with its liberal beliefs, had seen no immediate need for state intervention. England had led the industrial revolution and was at the height of its powers. The empire was being built and run by ex-public school boys. The working class worked and did not require education. There was no obvious need to extend the education service. Disagreements in England and Wales between the religious factions also contributed to the failure to set up universal education.

Towards the end of the nineteenth century, however, things were changing. Germany and the United States were overtaking the UK in industrial production. Both had compulsory state education. Fears began to be voiced about the lack of basic skills among the English working classes, sentiments which would echo through the next century. Would England be able to keep her world lead if the majority of workers were not educated? In addition there was a revolutionary spirit across Europe. Workers were beginning to demand more rights and the British ruling class began to fear that the uneducated masses in England might also take to the streets. The working classes needed to be disciplined and controlled and compulsory schooling could be the answer.

The introduction of the Factories Acts under Gladstone, a Liberal Prime Minister, ended the practice of very young children working in the market economy. This provided a space in their lives for formal education. Education up to this point had been left to the market. Those who could afford it got schooled, but the vast majority of children were denied any education at all. It became recognised that, left to the market, iniquities prevailed. In 1870 the state took it upon itself to take education out of the market and to provide a national education service financed through taxation. The state began to intervene to enforce change but change of a very definite kind, the outcome of which was to keep the poor in their place and maintain the privileges of the upper class.

SECONDARY EDUCATION FOR ALL: THE 1944 EDUCATION ACT

The next big step forward occurred with the introduction of Butler's 1944 Education Act. Education was to be compulsory for all pupils up to the age of fifteen. Pupils would no longer remain in elementary schools for their whole school life. At age eleven, after taking an examination, they would be routed to a suitable secondary school. This was known as the tri-partite system because secondary schools were divided into three types, grammar, technical and secondary moderns. The grammar schools were to provide a largely classical education, technical schools were to offer boys training in industrial and mechanical skills, and secondary modern schools were to cater for everyone else, teaching practical skills which would lead to suitable employment. In reality few technical schools ever opened and the vast majority, around 75 per cent of pupils, went to secondary modern schools.

The act is named after the Conservative politician, Rab Butler, but it was the product of a wartime coalition and reflects the social democratic principles which were prevalent at the time. After the devastating effects of two world wars the social democratic movement in the country at large was strong. World War II brought people together, masked class differences and produced a more communal spirit. Moreover, the winning of the war had been achieved through central planning with the state at the height of its power. There was a feeling at the end that everyone was entitled to a good free education and that it should be provided by the state.

COMPREHENSIVE EDUCATION: 1970S ONWARDS

From the early 1970s onwards there was a rapid change from the tripartite system to a comprehensive system of secondary education. This meant that all pupils in a given area would go to the same secondary school and that there would be no formal examinations for entry. The 1944 Act had allowed for this possibility but the Conservatives disliked the idea of comprehensive education and the number of comprehensive schools was only accelerated in 1967 when the Labour Party was in power. However, the change was not halted when the Conservatives returned to government, so that by 1981 over 90 per cent of schools[3] in England and Wales were comprehensive as were Scotland's. In a few areas of England grammar schools still exist to this day.

Grammar schools offered a route to qualifications and a place at university, but they took only a small proportion of the population. There was increasing worry about the waste of talent in pupils attending secondary modern schools, many of whom finished with few formal qualifications. Educationalists noted that the old class barriers still existed and grammar schools mostly drew on pupils from the middle classes. Although they afforded some opportunities for working class boys and girls, there still remained a class imbalance. Social democratic Europe educated all its pupils together irrespective of ability in the same school. This was the model the Labour party hoped to follow.

LOCAL MANAGEMENT OF SCHOOLS: THE 1988 EDUCATION ACT

Prior to the 1980s, education reform had centred around who should have access to education and how schools should be organised. Although these continued to be important issues, the focus of the1988 Education Act was different. It introduced the local management of schools (LMS). This meant that a budget was allocated by the local authority to each school and financial and managerial responsibility for the funds passed to the governors and head teacher. It was intended to give individual schools greater autonomy as well as providing for a more effective use of resources. It was also hoped that these changes would make schools more responsive to their clients, be they parents, children or local employers. Local authorities still retained some of the monies and were responsible for the provision of certain services.

Whilst giving the schools greater autonomy over their individual budgets, the 1988 Act also exerted much greater control over what schools actually did. It introduced a national curriculum which is discussed further in Chapter 4 and a much tighter inspection regime. Pupils were subject to standardised testing at ages seven, eleven and fourteen. These results together with information on GCSE performance were publicised, leading to the ranking of schools in any given authority, in effect producing league tables. The changes from 1988 onwards were brought into existence by a Conservative government which subscribed to neo-liberal tenets believing that the introduction of free market competition in education would produce greater choice for parents, greater efficiency in the spending of state money and improved examination results.

KEY ISSUES IN THE PROVISION OF SCHOOLING

There have been three main themes which have underpinned the development of state education in England and Wales. Who should have access to education, how should schools be organised and who should provide the service?

WHO SHOULD HAVE ACCESS TO EDUCATION?

The answer seems to us in the early part of the twenty-first century clear: everyone, irrespective of age, sex, ethnicity or social class. This was not the obvious answer for much of the twentieth century. The history of education has been one of a long struggle to achieve the limited level of universal access we now take for granted. The growth of state schooling has not just been a straightforward story of the increased access of more and more people to higher and higher levels of schooling. It has also been a battleground where social class, sex and ethnicity have all played their part. The seemingly straightforward pursuit of teaching and learning has been the arena where struggles for dominance and influence in society have been played out.

SCHOOLING AND CLASS

Educational achievement, whether measured in terms of GCSE results or university places, is still strongly related to pupils' social class. From the beginning of state education this was accepted as normal. England was, and is, a country of strong class differences. These were frequently thought of as unquestionable and inevitable, and education merely reflected the *status quo*. The earliest education Acts restricted access to secondary education for all except the comparatively well off and designated specific curricula for different classes of pupils. These issues are explored further in Chapter 4. After 1944 divisions remained, with grammar schools largely catering for middle class children. It was not until the 1970s and the introduction of comprehensive education that educational achievement became less related to social class, although class continues to be a powerful determinant of educational performance.

Social class has had a strong effect on parental attitudes and behaviour. Schooling, and the certification it gives, have long been seen as a way of gaining access to positions of power and prestige. The middle and upper classes have always understood the value of formal schooling and have sought to gain advantage in the competition for prestigious school and university places. The wealthy send their children to the well known private schools which offer a route into the more influential universities and ultimately the desired professions. A Sutton Report[4] states that over 60 per cent of Ministers in the 2010 government had attended fee-paying schools which educate only 7 per cent of the population.

SCHOOLING: GENDER AND ETHNICITY

The story of schooling has not just been a matter of class, however. Gender and ethnicity have also played a part. The twentieth century has been one which has seen a gradual increase in the rights of women and this has been reflected in education. In school it has been a fight for equal opportunities: for the right of girls to be taken seriously as learners, to be taught with materials that properly reflect female equality and to be given the same access as boys to all subjects on the curriculum. In the second half of the twentieth century, equality of opportunity became an important issue and the rights of ethnic minority pupils and special needs children were also addressed. Chapter 3 explores how this happened. Significant progress in relation to widening access has been made but it is uneven and children from poorer and certain ethnic backgrounds still remain disadvantaged in the education system.

HOW SHOULD SCHOOLING BE ORGANISED?

SEPARATE SECONDARY SCHOOLS: THE TRIPARTITE SYSTEM

Debate about how schools should be organised has continued ever since the 1870 Education Act and shows no signs of abating. A key question is whether children of secondary age are taught all together under one roof, or separated according to ability into different schools. In 1944 the latter option was preferred. There should be separate secondary schools for different groups of children based on their different abilities. This decision was based on evidence from the Norwood Committee which in 1943 produced a simple description of three types of pupil: the elite group, 'those interested in learning for its own sake', a second group, those with particular practical skills, who were mostly boys, described as those with 'an uncanny insight into the intricacies of mechanism' and finally the rest, 'those who deal more easily with concrete things than with ideas'. The elite group would go to grammar schools, those with practical skills to technical schools and the rest to secondary moderns. It's worth pausing at this point to ask oneself, 'Where would I fit?' Can I easily slot myself into one of those categories?

The decision as to the appropriate school for each child rested on an examination taken at age eleven, known as the eleven-plus. The exam included tests in English and maths but a central feature was the testing and measuring of intelligence. It was believed that an intelligence test would be able to predict how children would be likely to perform in their secondary schools. The concept of intelligence has been crucial to education in the UK. It has informed not only the organisation of schooling, but also the way pupils are taught and expectations as to what they will achieve. That being so, it is important to consider what is really known about intelligence.

THE CONCEPT OF INTELLIGENCE

'Intelligence' is a word that is freely used in conversation. Most of us employ it on a daily basis as fact: some people are intelligent, others less so. Television programmes and websites help people to measure their intelligence and competitions pit women against men, architects against plumbers with sometimes unpredictable results. Pupils' achievement in school is often attributed to their supposed intelligence levels. But despite considerable research we still do not have coherent accounts of what intelligence actually is. Most of our beliefs about intelligence come from ideas developed in the early twentieth century. Psychologists claimed to have identified a general mental ability called 'g' which, it was supposed, could be accurately measured. This general intelligence was an attribute of mind and was distinct from other qualities such as perception or memory. Moreover it was an all-purpose facility: if you were 'bright' you were bright in a general way and in school you would be likely to be good at a variety of subjects. Not only was intelligence *general*, it was also believed to be fixed and largely inherited. The precise level of anyone's intelligence could be determined through tests. These tests specified the limits of what children were likely to achieve, with far less being expected of those labelled less bright.

In the last twenty years or so research on the brain has radically changed the way intelligence is understood. There is now considerable controversy surrounding the notion of general intelligence. Some of our intelligence may indeed be inherited, but our life experience is now thought to have a profound effect upon intelligence. Scientists have suggested that experience alters the neurological paths in the brain and that intelligence changes and modifies as one progresses through life. These findings have not yet impacted on schooling in any significant way. When asked by the author to describe a class they had met for the first time, some teachers immediately divided the children into three groups, the bright, the middle-of-the road and the 'no hopers'. The old idea of innate intelligence has had a major effect on the categorising and labelling of children. It has contributed to many children growing up with the mistaken idea that they are not intelligent and cannot succeed in education.

CRITICISMS OF THE TRIPARTITE SYSTEM

Whilst the notion of general intelligence remained largely intact criticisms grew around the idea of intelligence testing. What exactly were the tests measuring? Children, it was found, could be coached for intelligence tests and as a result improve their performance and ultimate scores. What did this say about the measuring of innate abilities? Questions were also raised about the validity of the eleven–plus and the desirability of selection at age eleven. In theory if mistakes had been made in testing, there were opportunities to transfer school at thirteen, but in reality transfers were few and far between. The eleven–plus was a national exam, but standards differed across the UK. The percentage of students who were successful was related to the number of grammar schools places available in any particular area. Children in some areas had a four times greater chance of gaining a grammar school place than their peers elsewhere.[5] Girls performed consistently better than boys, but only received the same number of grammar school places.

COMPREHENSIVE SCHOOLS: BETTER OR WORSE?

Eventually demand for change came from all quarters. Dissatisfied parents, teachers, educationalists and politicians all voiced concern. It was thought that society as a whole would be better served if children were educated together in high quality local secondary schools. The majority of grammar schools were abolished and most children went to their local secondary school. Much of the rest of Europe was also comprehensive by this time. France, Italy and Spain taught all children together for the first years of secondary school although there was some differentiation in the later years The Scandinavian countries were completely comprehensive. Germany remained one of the few countries which still divided children into separate schools, but this did not happen before the pupils were twelve and, unlike the English system, there were frequent chances to change school later on. Moreover, the Germans in the northern European tradition prized practical, hands-on learning and many of the technical secondary schools were as valued as much as the more academic *Gymnasia*.

Since the advent of local comprehensive education the number of pupils gaining good GCSE results has increased year on year. Despite this there is dissatisfaction with the system from a number of different sources. From the beginning the aims surrounding comprehensive education were confused. Many parents saw comprehensive schools as a root to a more academic curriculum and increased certification for their children, but educationalists wanted an opportunity to broaden the curriculum and to do away with the division between academic and vocational subjects which the old system had enshrined. Needless to say neither group was happy. The hope that comprehensivisation would lead to children from different social classes mixing more freely was not realised. In some areas there was undoubtedly a mix of social classes in the new comprehensive schools, but in other places a hierarchy of schools evolved with the former grammar schools at the top of the pile and the former secondary modern schools in the less wealthy areas of town at the bottom. In the last thirty years the idea of comprehensive education has been questioned by both the Conservative party and New Labour. An already fragmented schooling system has become more uneven with the development of direct grant schools, academies, faith schools and, of late, free schools.

WHO SHOULD PROVIDE EDUCATION?

For the first 100 years or so of formal education in the UK it was generally accepted that the state should provide education. The advent of neo-liberal thinking in the 1980s changed all this, however, and subsequently both the Conservative and New Labour governments believed that education should be exposed to the market place and many aspects of education should be privatised. In addition in the UK, unlike in other countries, state schools have often been run by religious organisations and considerable controversy surrounds such arrangements.

THE CONCEPT OF PUBLIC SERVICE

In the first three-quarters of the twentieth century, in keeping with social democratic ideas, most UK politicians believed that education should be removed from the market place. Some continued paying privately for their children's education, but for everyone else, education was to be freely available. Associated with these ideas was the concept of public service. Education was regarded as a service not a product. Teaching was considered by many to be a socially useful job. It often meant lower wages and poorer working conditions than in the private sector, but teachers felt that by and large the work was worth doing. Difficult and challenging it might be, but it was intrinsically good and yielded personal satisfaction. It also provided job security. During this period the control of education was jointly shared between central government, local government and schools themselves. Schools frequently co-operated with each other, shared resources and did not compete for pupils. These ideas were radically challenged by Margaret Thatcher and successive

Conservative governments from the 1980s onwards who thought the market should be brought back into education. Many of the changes they subsequently enacted were also endorsed by New Labour.

EDUCATION AND MARKETISATION

In the 1980s a new strand of liberalism emerged which came to be known as *neo-liberalism*. Neo-liberals drew on the ideas of the US economist Milton Friedman. As early as 1955 he had criticised public services, including education. He maintained that a state school system having a monopoly on education was grossly inefficient. No incentive was given to teachers to innovate, to respond to the needs of the consumers or to cut costs. In order to rectify this, education needed to be submitted to the forces of the market place. Where possible the private sector should replace public sector provision. Parents and pupils were to become customers and consumers.

The Conservative government of the 1980s accepted the basic premises of neo-liberalism and set about changing education. In principle they favoured private schools and incentives were offered to parents to pay for their children's education. Spending on state schools was not prioritised and for a brief time they were referred to as council schools with the detrimental image these words suggested. Within the state sector, funding was related to the number of pupils on roll and schools were encouraged to compete with each other for customers. Parents were to be allowed to choose their child's secondary school and this process was facilitated by the publication of league tables which showed how each school was doing relative to its competitors. It was believed that this would lead to the better schools expanding, with the weaker schools losing pupils and eventually having to close their doors. Market competition, it was believed, would improve quality of provision and make schools more accountable for what they were doing.

The reforms of the 1980s led to the fragmentation of the education system. The introduction of LMS had allowed schools to be more independent, but a step further was taken when schools could apply to be grant-maintained. This meant that some schools opted out of local authority control altogether and then received their funds direct from central government. The trend continued with the introduction of city technology colleges, state schools in urban areas which are independently managed and mostly geared towards science and technology. Academies, secondary schools which were state-financed but privately run, were initially set up in areas where schooling was said to be failing, particularly the inner cities. In a strong departure from social democratic philosophy, New Labour under Tony Blair decided that failing schools could best be remedied by bringing in the private sector. In return for a small investment, private enterprise was permitted to run schools, decide curricula and pay staff on different scales from those decided nationally.

The 1988 Education Act also led to the privatisation of many school services. An example was school meals which came to be provided by private contractors. The advent of the market allowed pupils to choose their own meals, with the inevitable choice of burgers and chips. Far from giving a balanced diet, schools were providing, via private firms, food which was damaging to children's well-being. This was highlighted by Jamie Oliver in a series of television programmes which campaigned to bring healthy eating back to schools. The situation in England contrasted strongly with that of many other European countries which provided food to a high standard. Primary school children in Rome, for example, receive organic, wholesome food at a subsidised rate.

PROBLEMS WITH MARKETISATION

Making schools more independent through LMS has been seen as benefiting most schools, but other aspects of educational policy in the last twenty years have been seen as more problematic. Marketisation is based on the belief that education is a product which like any other should be subject to market forces. Marketisation however is an economic theory which does not sit easily with the concept of education. It assumes that the aim of schooling is straightforward, namely the securing of an educated and skilled work force, but this aim can be strongly challenged as subsequent chapters will show. It also assumes that schools are straightforward purveyors of knowledge and skills, but these ideas too are highly contestable. Introducing the market into education was supposed to make schools more efficient, but while it may be comparatively easy to gauge efficiency in the manufacture of biscuits, for example, it is difficult to determine with any precision whether schools are efficient or not.

Competition was also thought to encourage accountability and better exam results. Schools would strive to improve their pupils' performance in tests and public examinations since school funding would depend on attracting pupils. Undoubtedly this has had some impact on schooling: test and examination results have improved; but there is considerable debate over what this means. Competition has to some extent encouraged cheating. There is evidence of schools manipulating test results to gain a better position in the league tables and of teachers 'helping' pupils to produce good work. Moreover there is evidence that many teachers now 'teach to the test': securing as large a number as possible of good exam results has become a central aim for schooling. But is this the same as giving pupils a good education, or has it turned schools into narrowly focused accreditation factories?

Marketisation has tended to produce a fragmented education structure which is more geared to freedom of choice than to the creation of an equitable system. In this it is strongly aligned with the liberal ideas outlined earlier in the chapter. Europe, subject to the same economic shocks in the 1970s as the UK, has mostly retained a unified system. Norway and Sweden give larger amounts of money to less successful schools with the hope of improving them. The English on the other hand reward successful schools. Pupils from unified systems which afford little parental choice are doing noticeably better in international tests than are their counterparts in England. These findings are considered further in Chapter 6.

SCHOOLING AND RELIGION

A further strand in the discussion of who should be providing schooling in the UK covers the question of religion. It is difficult nowadays to view the UK as a particularly religious country. The numbers of people who say they regularly attend church have decreased rapidly since World War II, although membership of non-established Churches has grown. The influence of the Church on education however, has always been strong and it continues to have a major effect on present day schooling. In the nineteenth century many schools were run by religious organisations and these bodies have continued to have influence. This contrasts strongly with the experience of France and the United States where formal state education has always been secular, excluding where possible the specific interests of religious bodies. In the twentieth century the Church of England sought to influence the content of the curriculum and it was instrumental in the institution of regular religious assemblies in state schools. Far from decreasing, the influence of religion on education has grown. At the time of writing the government has been encouraging the creation of faith schools. It raises the question of the effect which religion has on our education system. This is considered further in Chapter 4.

PARENTAL CHOICE

It is understandable that all parents want the best for their children. For many this comes in the form of at least as good an education for their offspring as they themselves experienced. They are often prepared to go to great lengths and in some cases considerable sacrifice to ensure this happens. Some parents pay large sums of money for private education, and others frequently go to sizeable lengths to secure the state places they desire. Stephen Ball, in *Class Strategies and the Education Market*, has documented much of this. Middle class people are more in a position to choose where to live and have tended to buy houses close to desirable schools. Some parents have even been known to fake residencies or to rent rooms in houses adjacent to their preferred school. He points out that the introduction of the market into education has been of benefit to the middle classes, although it also presents them with challenges, an example of which is the annual difficulty in securing first choice school places. Most of the challenges, however, Ball maintains, middle class parents are well able to meet. They are used to working on schools to secure their desired ends.

There is ample evidence to suggest that what exists is choice for some parents and the illusion of choice for the rest. Working class parents are much less likely to be able to choose where they live or to have the know-how to make their voice heard in the education system. If the allocation of school places occurs in a competitive environment where status wealth and know-how matter, the middle classes will invariably triumph. This does not mean that the middle class are bad or exploitative. It does mean that a system which allows competition and choice between schools and which funds successful schools more than failing schools is likely to be a system which perpetuates inequalities.

HIGHER EDUCATION

THE GROWTH OF UNIVERSITIES

It would be wrong to leave this history of schooling in the UK without considering the extraordinary expansion of university education in the twentieth century. Universities have existed in the UK since medieval times. Oxford and Cambridge opened in the fourteenth century and by the end of the sixteenth century there were five more similar institutions. Little then happened until the nineteenth century when four more universities including the University of London were given charters. The dawn of the twentieth century marked the arrival of six more institutions which became known as 'redbrick' universities. On the recommendation of the Robbins Report in 1963, further expansion came with the opening of 'new' universities in the 1960s and the arrival of the Open University which taught by distance learning. The final development came after 1992 when polytechnics were given university titles and degree-awarding powers. This was gradually extended to Colleges of Higher Education many of which had developed from teacher training colleges.

All universities, except the University of Buckingham, are financed by the state, although this looks likely to change in the future. The universities of Oxford and Cambridge are also financed through private endowments. Students in England and Wales pay fees for their tuition, although in Wales the fees are capped and therefore lower. Scottish students do not pay fees provided they attend Scottish universities. The fees to date have been subsidised from taxation but this has now ceased, with students in the future being required to pay the full cost. In the UK a hierarchy of universities exits. This relates to their history and to their research reputations: roughly speaking the older the university the more prestige it has. Research output varies across the sector but it is becoming increasingly concentrated in a few of the older universities.

ACCESS TO UNIVERSITIES

Until the 1960s and the Committee on Higher Education (Robbins) Report British universities were highly elitist. In the early 1960s only 5 per cent of school-leavers went to university, and few of these were women who had a long fight to gain access to university education. Universities such as Oxford and Cambridge allowed entry to girls in the 1920s, but it was 1948 before Cambridge allowed women to graduate with a degree. Jane Robinson in her book *Bluestockings* shows that in letters to home, female students gave numerous stories of abuse by male fellow undergraduates. These included an account of riots in Cambridge in 1897 when Cambridge male undergraduates objected strongly to women becoming members of the university, stringing up an effigy in protest. There were also accounts of professors refusing to teach female classes.

The last twenty years have seen a massive expansion in higher education. More than 30 per cent of eighteen-year-olds are now estimated to be in full time education.[6] This is still a smaller percentage than most of the rest of Europe, Japan and the United States. As with schooling, widening participation has been encouraged and the advent of Access Courses in the late 1980s allowed students without standard qualifications to gain university places.

PURPOSE OF THE UNIVERSITY

Many original medieval European universities were run by the Catholic Church, but in the nineteenth century the modern university emerged throughout Europe with a strong belief in academic freedom. Universities were there to carry out research and to discover knowledge which was rational and scientific. This inevitably led to a robust critique of religious and other belief systems. British universities were strongly in this tradition. Although universities in the UK are state-funded, 'academic freedom' means that the government is not allowed to determine the universities' curriculum or research topics.

Universities in the UK are changing. The old ideas of their being seats of learning where the battle for truth is fought out and a critical approach to the world adopted is fading. As with schooling, the state is looking to universities to fill the skills gap and the number of vocational courses is increasing. They are becoming more job-focused. There has been a massive increase in funding for the universities. As times get harder and funding is more tightly scrutinised, the question of value for money is likely to get stronger. It will set the tone for what is to come and the degree to which universities are able to control their own futures. Again, it is the market, rather than the government, which will be in control as students select their preferred university and courses.

CONCLUSION

This chapter has examined the development of schooling in the UK in the last hundred and forty years. It has noted that most schooling is state controlled and affected by the ideological beliefs of the political party in power. The story of education in the UK has been one of increasing access for more and more pupils, but decisions about eligibility have frequently been based on a flawed understanding of intelligence and potential. Since the 1980s, education has moved from being considered a service to being a marketable product. We live at present in a society which puts personal choice above the needs of the wider society. The freedom of the parent to secure advantage for their child through choice of schooling has become the hallmark of our society. Education, rather than being a social good, is seen more as a personal investment. Its aim: to bring high returns to the individual in the form of future salaries and increased life opportunities. This has helped create a schooling system which lacks balance and bestows benefits on some but not others. Do we neglect the wider good at our peril? Is education contributing to the growth of a kind of society we may not be comfortable with?

WHAT ARE THE PURPOSES OF SCHOOLING?

THE PURPOSES MAY SEEM OBVIOUS

Schools exist to teach basic skills and prepare pupils for future employment. In order to function in the modern world children need to be literate, numerate and have good IT skills. They also eventually need actual jobs and school has a role in making pupils ready for the world of work. Schools should also teach pupils to behave properly and should discipline them when they misbehave. These views have been supported by successive governments throughout the twentieth century. Politicians in recent years have strengthened these beliefs by linking education to the economic health of the nation. The world is changing and in order to compete in global markets, they say, the country needs workers with new and improved competences who are versatile and able to adjust to changing circumstances. Thus the purposes of education seem beyond debate.

However this is an insufficient answer. While few would deny the importance of teaching basic skills and giving children decent manners, there are other roles which schooling performs. Education is one of the ways through which children learn about the society in which they live and its core values. It can lead to social cohesion. It can help create a society in which most feel at home. In addition education has been seen as the vehicle through which young people improve their lot in life, with some ending up more 'successful' than their parents. Finally, and perhaps most important, it can offer the prospect of personal development for the individual and social transformation for society as a whole. Jobs may be important, but the development of self-knowledge and the ability to think critically remain the hallmarks of a civilised society.

In order to understand what schooling is all about, and what it might look like in future, it is necessary to look in more depth at the purposes of education and to understand that these may not be as straightforward as they initially seemed. Moreover, the purposes sometimes conflict with each other, and in national educational policy and at school level such conflicts need to be resolved.

SCHOOLING FOR WORK

TEACHING RELEVANT KNOWLEDGE AND SKILLS

Schools have long had a role in preparing pupils for work. They have done this through the knowledge and skills which are taught and through the final certification which is awarded at the end of schooling. In the early history of state education there was a concern with teaching numeracy and literacy and this has largely remained. Even as late as the 1980s employers were suggesting that school leavers were failing in these basic skills. Since then successive governments have prioritised these subjects and introduced standard assessment tasks (SATs) to determine the levels pupils are achieving at any particular age. Until recently there has been a steady rise in performance in literacy although this may now have peaked. Some schools have performed better than others on national tests and they have been rewarded by governments giving them more independence.

EDUCATION AND THE KNOWLEDGE ECONOMY

Are the skills currently taught in school the right skills for the future however? New Labour, whilst in power, suggested that there was a need for education to respond to the growth of the knowledge economy and the spread of globalisation. Tony Blair argued that education had to be 'modernised' both in the way it was organised and in the skills it was delivering. 'An army of skilled technical experts' would be needed in order for the UK to fully take part in the knowledge economy. But what was meant by the term 'knowledge economy'? The term is difficult to define but it purports to describe the way advanced industrial economies are being transformed from industries dependent on raw materials and manufacturing to industries based on the creation and trading of knowledge. Jobs in the UK, it is argued, are becoming largely professional, semi-professional and managerial rather than manual, and education needs to adapt to deal with this. What pupils now need are problem-solving and entrepreneurial skills.

The UK economy is undoubtedly changing. Recent years have seen a huge growth in the service industries such as retail, transport, hospitality and care, but is this the same as a growth in knowledge-based companies? The real economy is more complex than the term 'knowledge economy' might suggest and forcing the education system to fit a particular idea of the economy might be counter-productive. This is just one example of the difficulties in trying to tailor schools to meet the needs of 'the economy'.

QUESTIONING WHAT THE ECONOMY IS DOING

Skills that help with getting jobs will be applauded by most people, but is the teaching of work-based competencies the only thing schools have to do in relation to the economy? In Western societies we live in capitalist states which have produced many advances in goods and services and have contributed to the transformation of people's lives, but there have been ill effects too. Current capitalism it is argued, has benefited the wealthy at the expense of the less privileged; in recent years in some countries, particularly the United States and the UK, it has led to a massive widening in the gap between the rich and the poor. It has led to the exploitation of people in the Third World. It has increasingly tended to produce goods which people do not necessarily need but are persuaded to buy. The side effects of this are waste and inefficiency together with increasing consumption of the world's dwindling resources.

Whether one agrees with such criticisms of capitalism or not, it is of fundamental importance that pupils understand the economic world in which they live. John Dewey and Michael Apple, US educationalists, have both at different times argued that, far from supporting the economy, schools should show pupils how the economy actually works and who benefits from it. Schools should have at the core of their mission the task of countering the private interests of the economy. The economy need not be a fixed structure into which everyone has to be slotted. In a world of climate change, peak oil and reduced natural resources schools have a duty to foster individuals who will debate, question and challenge, economic orthodoxy rather than passive consumers.

IMPROVING THE ECONOMY

Politicians have sought to draw a link between what goes on in school and how the economy performs. But is it correct to make this link? The relationship between schooling and economic performance is difficult to gauge. A large number of other factors contribute to economic well being, including the level of investment, the availability of credit and the competitive nature of local business. Recent banking failures and the power of certain banks to hold the nation to ransom are a powerful testament to this factor. Ha-Joon Chang in his recent book *Twenty-three Things They Don't Tell You about Capitalism* has argued that there is little evidence to suggest that more education in itself makes a country richer. Contrary to popular belief, he maintains, better maths and science results do not result in better economic performance. On the other hand a report in 2010 produced by the Organisation for Economic Co-operation and Development (OECD), *The High Cost of Low Educational Performance* found a strong relationship between economic growth and the development of pupils' cognitive skills. It suggested that relatively small increases in the skills of a nation's workers could have a very positive effect on economic well-being. So it seems that investing in education, as the UK has in recent years, is insufficient on its own. Much depends on the kind of education system being promoted. These considerations are discussed further in Chapter 6.

PREPARING THE YOUNG PSYCHOLOGICALLY FOR WORK

Finally, schools do not just provide the knowledge and skills which might help pupils get jobs. They go further than this. Bowles and

Gintis in their work *Schooling in Capitalist America* looked at US schools in 1976 and used Marxist theory to claim that school was preparing children psychologically for work. Capitalism, they argued, needs a subservient work force which will not question the economic structure or an individual's role in it. Schooling performs this job. What happens at school corresponds with what happens at work. Workers need to keep strict time and obey the boss, and schooling teaches these skills. Motivation is encouraged by rewards such as stars and accreditation and this prepares pupils for the competitive world of work. School also differentiates between pupils, preparing some of them for jobs higher up the scale and others for more menial tasks. From the beginning children are channelled into the appropriate route for them and this relates strongly to their gender, race and class. Revisiting their work in 2001 they maintained that in essence their original findings were still correct.

This was America, however. Could Bowles and Gintis have any relevance for the UK? Basil Bernstein, writing around the same time in the UK, challenged their views. He maintained that if preparation for work was the main function of schools they were obviously demonstrably failing in view of the large number of children who were truanting and challenging the system. He did however concede that in some ways schooling was strongly connected to the world or work.

GOOD BEHAVIOUR: THE PROCESS OF SOCIALISATION

Beyond teaching children skills and knowledge which will be useful in the future, schools also have a recognized role in teaching pupils codes of behaviour. We are not born social beings, although we may have a strong propensity to be so. From the very beginning infants are taught about the needs of others. Through interaction with their parents and other adults they became aware of what is acceptable behaviour in any given society. This process is called 'socialisation'. It begins in the home and is continued at school.

The French sociologist Emile Durkheim, writing at the very beginning of state schooling, felt that a school's role in the socialisation process was crucial. He argued that schools are there primarily to control children for the benefit of everyone. Schooling has the important role of turning a child into someone who can consider the needs of others. School is thus transforming the egotistic child into someone who can coexist comfortably with other people, and this process is crucial for the survival of all of us. Durkheim agreed with Bowles and Gintis that there is a relationship between what happens in school and what happens in society. Rules in school prepare a child for behaviour in the adult world. For Bowles and Gintis this was problematic, while Durkheim saw it as a good thing.

Taken at face value most of us can probably support these features of socialisation. Initial ideas of teaching politeness and concern for others seem fairly uncontroversial. Children enter some form of schooling usually in the shape of nursery education at a very early age. They often come from a setting in which they have been the centre of the carer's attention, but it is important for them to become aware of the needs of others and to learn that they are one amongst many all with equal claims to consideration. Schooling performs this role to a lesser or greater extent. Children learn that it's wrong to hit others and that they must wait their turn in getting teacher attention. The process of socialisation, however, does not just cover politeness and good manners: it goes much deeper and contributes to a fundamental understanding of who we are and what our identity is. Nowhere is this more important than in relation to gender.

UNDERSTANDING THE CONCEPT OF GENDER

Women have played various roles down the ages and have often been prominent leaders of their day. In different cultures, they have often done different jobs. In Russia, for example, there have always been many more female engineers *per capita* than in the UK. How can this be? It cannot be attributed solely to biological differences. The concept of gender suggests that individuals may be born male or female but different societies have different expectations as to how men and women should think and behave. In other words, what counts as feminine or masculine behaviour varies from one society to the next. In any given place or time individuals learn how to behave in a manner which is acceptable for their sex. To return to the subject of engineering, for example, in some societies, such as the UK, it is considered to be essentially a masculine pursuit. This has knock-on effects for the numbers of women choosing engineering as a career.

GENDER ROLES: AN EXAMPLE OF SOCIALISATION

We learn our gender identity through the process of socialisation. This teaches us appropriate behaviour for our particular sex and this begins from birth. The first question people ask on being told of a new arrival is frequently, 'Is it a girl or boy?' Cards and presents are sent and these come in the appropriate colours, pink for girls and blue for boys. Indeed the last twenty-five years have shown an unprecedented rise in this stereotyping, so much so that there is almost no other colour choice. The clothing carries a message about what is expected of each sex. Lauren Richardson Walum in her book *The Dynamics of Sex and Gender* describes experiments in which the same child was dressed alternatively in pink or blue clothes and the reactions of adults then noted. What happened next demonstrated that people reacted to the colour of the clothing and not the child. When dressed in pink the baby was treated gently, cuddled and cooed over. When dressed in blue the same baby was more roughly handled and allowed far more movement. Toy catalogues likewise list toys by sex, the pages often edged and presented in the 'appropriate' colour. They show dolls, prams, shopping and cooking items for girls, cars, swords and construction toys for boys. Children are encouraged from the beginning to learn the roles that are likely to be demanded of them in life.

Gender is a subtle and powerful determinant of behaviour. Most people, with some notable exceptions, do not want to be perceived to be out of keeping with their gender. Girls on the whole want to be thought of as feminine and boys as masculine. Even if at a rational level girls and boys reject limitations which gender stereotypes place on them, at a subconscious level these determinants remain very strong.

SCHOOLING AND GENDER ROLES

Schools can either strengthen or challenge gender roles. There are a number of indices which suggest where an individual school stands in relation to this. From staff room agendas to classroom wall displays, every area of schooling carries a hidden message. In looking at the classroom one can scrutinise the wall displays and askwho are they depicting: are men and women, girls and boys equally prominent? Do the jobs that people are depicted doing reflect or challenge gender stereotypes? Likewise one can enquire who is participating the most in the classroom? To whom is the teacher giving attention? In most classrooms it is the boys who have been dominating the public arena and getting the most teacher attention.

Classroom materials are also important. Early reading books all contain important messages about what roles adults and children play in society. A trawl through current texts for example shows that men are given more employment opportunities than women. A dearly loved favourite by Judith Kerr, *The Tiger who Came to Tea*, shows the mother at home and the father at work with their strong accompanying roles. Of course it depends how the book is read and this is true of all curriculum materials used in school. Many materials, especially those promoted by businesses and government come with a hidden message. The value of the education depends on the quality of the discussion in the classroom.

SOCIAL CONTROL

Most of us accept the need for society to produce tolerant human beings who are willing to think of the needs of others and not to engage in too many belligerent acts. To this end we might endorse the role of the school in socialisation. But how far should this process go? This example observed by the author illustrates the lasting effect of socialisation. A secondary head teacher is standing outside her room. At the far end is a young lad, clearly out of class and perhaps 'up to no good'. The head teacher in her strongest voice roars, 'What do you think you are doing?' There is a large bang. Unnoticed by the head, two men are in the process of installing a soft drinks machine in the corridor. They drop it on the floor and immediately begin a process of abject apology. 'We're very sorry. We asked permission in the office … ' The lad takes the opportunity to make a quick getaway. Why were a couple of adult men in their forties so intimidated? What effect had schooling had on these men that they react so when confronted with a head teacher? When does socialisation become social control?

SCHOOLS AS INSTITUTIONS

The eminent sociologist Irving Goffman in his book *Asylums* looked at the ways in which institutions such as mental hospitals, prisons and concentration camps control their inmates. He called them 'total institutions' engaged in what he called 'an assault on the self': an attempt to take away an inmate's individuality. They do this by a variety of methods. All inmates wear a strict uniform, show obedience and deference to their handlers. Certain postures, movements and stances are forbidden. Residents are deprived of privacy and often subjected to humiliating acts. The ultimate purpose of the process is the exercise of social control and the production of individuals who are unlikely to challenge the regime. Indeed many occupants quickly become institutionalised: unable to think or act on their own without institutional support. This theme was picked up in the popular film *The Shawshank Redemption*. Prisoners like Brooks Hatlen become so institutionalised that they are unable to function outside the prison.

Schools are institutions in which most people spend a good deal of their formative years. But surely they cannot be described as 'total institutions'? Children go home at three-thirty. They are not there at weekends, except of course for children in boarding schools, and they have long holidays away. Nevertheless, when Goffman's analysis is applied to UK schools there are some striking similarities. Children in the UK, unlike most of the rest of the world, frequently wear uniform. Uniform is regularly checked and pupils penalised if they have transgressed. It is a source of considerable tension in school. It raises the question why pupils are required to look alike with little attention paid to their individuality. Obedience and deference are also encouraged in school, although they may not always be achieved. Time is strictly controlled. When else does one have to gain consent to go to the toilet, except in the most repressive of regimes? Red, in *The Shawshank Redemption*, constantly asks permission to use the lavatory even after he has been released. Schools are notorious for their lack of privacy, and humiliating experiences are a significant part of school life for some pupils.

Of course it is a considerable exaggeration to compare schools with prisons. There are significant differences and in some schools all attempts to control pupils in these ways fail. Nevertheless the idea of institutionalisation remains a powerful one. Many pupils arrive in university anxious about even speaking in a class, let alone expressing a controversial opinion. People in all walks of life, and particularly at work, have a fear of standing out or of challenging current beliefs. 'Groupthink' often takes over: people think alike without much questioning. It happens even at the national level. The Chilcott Inquiry into the Iraq war suggested that Cabinet members tended for various reasons not to question the Prime Minister. Everyone can think of times when things said should not have gone unchallenged and it is important to question the degree to which our early lives and our experiences of schooling have made us acquiescent to the given line and unwilling to stand up and be counted.

THE VIEWS OF PUPILS

Perhaps, however, children should have the last say about whether or not they are experiencing school as controlling and institutionalising. Catherine Burke and Ian Grosvenor in *The School I'd Like* report on the views of children collected in 1967 and 2001. In 1967 the *Observer* newspaper asked for comments from pupils on the school they'd like to go to. A selection of these was put together in a book by Edward Blishen. In 2001 the *Guardian* repeated the experiment. Once again, pupils were invited to imagine and describe their ideal school. Large numbers of young people responded and their replies were analysed by Burke and Grosvenor. They drew on Blishen's earlier work, comparing his findings with their more recent ones. Despite there being thirty-five years between the two reports, the message remained the same: pupils are unequivocal. Secondary students in particular condemn the institutional and authoritarian aspects of school life and liken school to prison. They feel like caged animals, hostile beings which the school wishes to civilise. They are not trusted. Teachers are not prepared to listen. Throughout the books pupils challenge the institutional aspects of schooling, from the shape and organisation of the buildings to the structure of teaching and learning.

SCHOOLS AND SOCIAL COHESION

LEARNING ABOUT THE SOCIETY WE LIVE IN

A major role for education has always been teaching the young about the world they live in. It is a way of passing on information from one generation to the next; but more than this, it is a way of preserving particular cultures and traditions. The young are inducted into the values and beliefs which an individual society holds dear. Aboriginal stories, Chinese revolutionary fables and English fairy tales, are all about teaching young children the ideas and values which are important to their society. Most education systems also teach history and some teach religious education, both of which include some account of how a nation has evolved. This knowledge has important outcomes. How a people understands its history has a direct bearing on how it sees itself in the world and how it may conduct itself in the future. These subjects are never neutral: they come with values attached which can be beneficial or not to the society concerned. The UK is a multicultural society with pupils of many different ethnic origins. To what degree can a school present a story of the UK which makes sense to all pupils and gives each child a sense of ownership? This is discussed in Chapter 4.

It would be wrong to underestimate the power of schooling: it has the potential to help create a world which could be life enhancing, emancipatory and positive, or diminishing, enslaving and negative. Children spend endless hours in school. Even when they appear turned off and disaffected, or are in strong opposition to school, they still receive and assess countless messages from teachers and schooling that are long lasting.

A CLASH OF VALUES?

Beyond teaching basic common courtesy and respect for the views of others, how do schools deal with more complicated values? What happens if the values of the home are different from the values of the school? How is this to be dealt with? Ethnic minority students have often detailed the problems they have experienced at school in relation to this. A professor of education at Berkeley, California, Eugene Garcia in *Student Cultural Diversity,* wrote a graphic account of his own experience of education. Born to a Hispanic family in the southern states he grew up in a farming family. The demands that this placed upon him as a child were not understood at school. His name was anglicised and he was not expected to do exceptionally well. Against all odds he succeeded and wrote an impassioned plea for schools to be more conversant with children's origins and to show respect for home values. In doing this he recounted a story told by his father. 'How does a tree survive the bitter cold of winter and the harsh heat of summer?' Answer: 'Good strong roots. From a fallen tree, anyone, everyone can make firewood.'

Understanding and respecting family roots and values is obviously important for schools, but education has a job also to do in challenging values. One of the original meanings of 'education' is 'to lead forth', and education at its best needs to challenge parochial and xenophobic views. It opens the student to a wider world and gives him or her, the ability to review beliefs and values in the light of new evidence.

CREATING GOOD CITIZENS

An attempt at promoting social cohesion has come in recent years with the introduction in schools in England and Wales of Education for Citizenship. This is a part of the curriculum which outlines and asks pupils to take account of their rights and duties as citizens. It sounds admirable but what counts as a good citizen? A good citizen is someone who pays their taxes, abides by the laws of the land and shows some concern for his/her fellow human beings. But is this sufficient? Might the main aim of citizen education be just to encourage compliance? Could it be just an extension of social control? Education needs to help pupils discuss and understand the full implications of being an active citizen.

PROMOTING EQUAL OPPORTUNITIES

Beyond making individuals employable, successive governments, especially those in the left-of-centre tradition, have claimed to see education as a way of creating more equality of opportunity and have tried, with limited success to influence the *status quo*. But what is meant by the term 'equality of opportunity'?

EQUAL TREATMENT FOR ALL

Equality of opportunity is a slogan which practically everybody subscribes to. Politicians from across the political spectrum have argued in favour of equal opportunities. The phrase however means different things to different people. Originally it stood for equal treatment for everyone. All pupils were to be treated in like manner with no discrimination and it was up to the individual to take advantage of the opportunities on offer but this overlooks the fact that different people have different needs, and respect for equality does not involve treating everyone in the same way. Pupils with physical disabilities for example may require help to avail themselves of the opportunities on offer to their able-bodied peers. The 'equal treatment' philosophy when used in school had at its basis the belief that minority groups should adapt to the prevailing culture: everyone should be the same. No attempts were made to include a multicultural perspective on history, for example, and ethnic minority pupils were virtually invisible in school, following a script which in every way excluded them. This was part of a tradition which believed that school should ignore pupils' roots, thus liberating them from the cultural constraints of their home background.

EQUAL ACCESS FOR ALL

Another way of looking at equal opportunities is to ensure that all pupils have equal access to everything that schooling has to offer. A raft of legislation under the Labour governments of the 1970s attempted to increase the opportunities for pupils who had been marginalised in, or excluded from, mainstream schooling. The Sex Discrimination Act of 1975, for example, made it illegal to discriminate against either sex in access to classes or courses. It widened opportunities for girls and focused teachers' attention on the degree to which classroom practice was often male-orientated. This Act was rapidly followed by legislation concerned with the experiences of ethnic minority children and children with disabilities. The Acts enabled teachers and educationalists to change current practice so that an inclusive curriculum, better classroom interaction and less prejudice were a more widespread feature of education. In the same period the introduction of comprehensive schooling was intended to make more opportunities available. Under the Conservatives in 1988, the introduction of the National Curriculum ensured that all pupils learned the same subjects up to the age of sixteen. The act included some recognition that there are differences between cultures: not everyone is the same and due respect should be given to the traditions and beliefs of all pupils and communities.

Whilst equal opportunities legislation has undeniably changed the school experience for many pupils, the problems remain deep-seated and not easily influenced by changes in legislation. Pupils with ability from poorer homes are still far less likely to be successful in education than their more wealthy peers. Girls may be doing well in school, but are not translating this into job success. The glass ceiling appears to be strengthening. Ethnic minority students still encounter racism. This raises questions as to the degree to which education can compensate for inequalities in society.

EQUAL SHARES

This final approach to equal opportunities maintains that true opportunity cannot be said to be in place unless all groups in society have an equal chance of success. Equal opportunities would be a reality when women and members of ethnic minority groups were equally represented in the corridors of power. At the present time in the UK only 22 per cent of MPs are female, which makes Britain No. 50 in the international league table of women in parliament. Only four of the twenty-nine Ministers who can currently attend Cabinet meetings are women.[1] Less that 10 per cent of high-court judges are women.[2] Women are still not included in the upper echelons of the Church of England and the Pope has called moves to create women bishops religious criminality. Ethnic minorities fare if anything worse, except in religious organisations. There is still major inequality in relation to pay. Advocates of equal shares argue that what matters is equality of outcome and not just equality of opportunity. In a just society ensuring that this happens is the collective responsibility of everyone.

At school there are many barriers to success and these are considered in Chapter 3. In deciding the extent to which a society had achieved equal opportunities one would need to look at the effects of a policy and not just at its intentions. Giving children equal access to educational services, for example, does not remove the substantial obstacles that some pupils encounter. Ha-Joon Chang, in his book on capitalism, points out that equality of opportunity regarded in this way is a myth. If some pupils have to run the race with sandbags attached to their legs, the fact that everyone starts from the same point makes little difference to the outcome. Equality of opportunity would only exist if efforts were made to remove the sandbags.

'WHERE DO I STAND?'

We all need to ask where we stand in relation to this question. Politicians of all persuasions have different beliefs about equality. Many have pinned their faith on the freedom of the individual to make their own choices. They have tended to reject all but minimal state intervention to secure equality. Given enough determination, all can succeed. These arguments are seductive. Most people want to believe that they can succeed if they try hard enough, but evidence suggests this is not so. For many choice is illusory, particularly if they face discrimination. Research by Leni Wiki, in 2005 for example found that in selecting potential MPs parties tend to choose men. In addition the culture of parliament, the socialisation process women have previously experienced, the problems of child care and lack of finance all combine to prevent success. There is no level playing field. Hard effort does not guarantee success.

MERITOCRACY

The post-war period has seen the growth of the idea of meritocracy. It is a concept rooted in assumptions that we cannot all be equal. Some will end up more powerful than others, but power in society should go to those who have superior abilities demonstrated through academic and other achievements, rather than through the possession of wealth, social status, gender or race. We should all have the opportunity to succeed. Those who have ability and work hard should be rewarded. Up to a point this position seems reasonable. Most people feel that those who make an effort should be rewarded. However, looked at more closely, once again difficulties arise. Firstly academic success is currently measured on the basis of examination results. Is performance in tests a valid way of measuring merit or would a wider system of assessment be more appropriate? Are those who underperform or fail lacking altogether in merit? These questions are reviewed more fully in Chapter 5.

Under a system of meritocracy, people who have become successful free themselves from social criticism; they become untouchable. They gain huge salaries and bonuses which both they and the wider public think they merit. This has been obvious in recent years with the rise of celebrity culture, sports stars and the like. It has also featured prominently in the recent banking crisis. The position of such people is unchallengeable because unlike their predecessors, who inherited their wealth and status, these people *merit* their rewards. On the other side of the coin, those who are not successful are held personally responsible for their failure. The term 'meritocracy' was first coined by Michael Young in a satirical book entitled *The Rise of the Meritocracy*. He had intended that this writing should act as a warning for the future. Revisiting his work in 2001, he expressed alarm that his counsels had not been heeded. A meritocracy, much proclaimed by politicians, he said could in fact be producing a far more rigid system of inequality than any that has gone before, and the upper class which subsequently emerges may be harder to dislodge than the old class–based on money and status.

PERSONAL DEVELOPMENT AND SOCIAL TRANSFORMATION

EDUCATION FOR PERSONAL DEVELOPMENT

This final purpose of schooling may well be the most important. Education at its best opens up a new world for students. It takes them on a voyage, presents them with challenges and ultimately transforms them. The children in *The School that I'd Like* were clear about this. They wanted an education which was exciting, relevant to living in a global community and personally empowering. Education should be enjoyable. It should foster creativity and engage all of them, their bodies, brains, minds and emotions. Many pupils express the need to enjoy learning and to get personal satisfaction from a course of study. A strong element of this often involves personally taking charge of one's own learning, deciding on a direction. This has always been an important element in in education and lifelong learning. It suggests an approach w] currently at odds with schooling in England where the curriculum is highly prescribed and centrally conceived, and where personal choice about the path learning should take is minimal. It demonstrates the ways in which the different purposes of education may come into conflict with each other.

A recent development in both schools and universities has been to write courses with prearranged learning outcomes. At the beginning of each course details are given of what the pupil should have learned by the end of their study. This is obviously helpful to both teachers and pupils. Teachers have a focus which stops them drifting away from the topic and pupils have a good map of where they should be going. However, it can be argued that specifying outcomes shuts down opportunities. Maybe the most exciting learning occurs when we don't know where we are going. It is perhaps the unexpected twists and turns on the way, the intellectually dangerous areas we encounter and the opportunities for discovering things which are off the map which ultimately lead to personal development.

MAKING A DIFFERENCE

Education has never been solely about getting a job or pursuing self-interest; it has always had other altruistic aims. Generations of teachers have been concerned with making a difference in pupils' lives, helping students take hold of their futures and ultimately helping raise individuals who will contribute to making the world a better place. The great educationalist Ted Wragg said that teachers change the world. There is he said, no more powerful calling than this. Education can thus be seen as a vehicle for social change.

Pupils too want to make a difference. The contributions of children to the pupil parliaments in England and their ideas for saving the world profiled in the International Children's Conferences on the Environment have demonstrated great enthusiasm for tackling difficult questions and finding credible solutions. As the challenges facing everyone, particularly those relating to climate change and peak oil, grow, then the demand for education in such matters, and the wherewith all to deal with intractable problems, is likely to increase.

EDUCATION FOR SOCIAL TRANSFORMATION

The sociologist Emile Durkheim rejected the idea that education could transform society, believing instead that society got the schooling it deserved. Using a Durkheimian perspective, the problems which politicians have highlighted with education – poor teachers, undisciplined pupils, simpler tests and so on – are rooted in society. Schooling merely reflects this world. Other educators have believed that education does have the power to transform individuals and ultimately society itself. The Brazilian educator Paulo Freire demonstrated that by engaging with social injustice and recognizing where power in society lies, students could transform both their own attitudes and the attitudes in society generally. In this way education could offer hope for the future. These ideas are explored further in Chapter 6.

UNIVERSITIES

UNIVERSITIES AND THE WORLD OF WORK

Universities in the past, particularly the more prestigious ones, considered themselves largely immune to government policies, but this is altering. They have had to change in response to the closer relationship posited between education and the economy. Not a bad thing, one might think. Students need good employment at the end of the day. Universities obviously must develop skills which help students understand what is needed to secure good jobs on graduation. Recently there has been a national drive for universities to permeate their courses with information about future jobs, careers and skills which might benefit students. Ha-Joon Chan however has argued that although higher education is valuable, more people with university degrees do not significantly affect productivity. Whatever the reality of the situation, in a highly unstable and uncertain world, producing graduates who can both adapt to the world of work and problematise it remains crucial.

RECONCILING CONFLICTING AIMS

The list of aims for schooling is formidable and they are in some ways irreconcilable. How are we to make sense of this? Which are the more important aims and who decides? It seems logical that an understanding of education in schools should begin with a discussion on what the aims of schooling are. But in recent years this kind of discussion has been largely absent. Whether in the media, governmental discussions or educational discourse the aims of education have become largely subsumed under the general aim of supporting the economy. So important has become the necessity to compete on a global scale that all other considerations have been set aside.

Most people recognise the importance of getting jobs, but there has been of late a palpable discontent with the nature and extent of work. We live and work in an environment which is rapidly and unpredictably changing. The work of sociologists like Richard Sennett has highlighted the effects of a changing economy on the work force at large. Workers are now more likely to lose their jobs as a result of 'downsizing' and 'flexible capitalism'; rapid change is creating a sense of insecurity and lack of anchorage. People are beginning to question the nature and necessity of work in ways which they perhaps have not done in the past. Together with this have come discussions about work/life balance and the effects of work on family life. Positive psychology has been pointing out what many people already know, that money and consumables are no guarantee of happiness. The move towards a discussion of what constitutes quality of life involves the question of the role of education in relation to this. Has the stress on work-related skills been too great? Should more time in schooling be spent on helping children secure a wider perspective which re-emphasises the importance of leisure and does not make the acquisition of wealth the main impetus for education?

CONCLUSION

This chapter has looked at the main purposes Of schooling and questioned the degree to which education should be considered as a preparation for work. Whilst providing pupils with vital skills, schooling would essentially be failing both students and society at large if it did not provide a critique of the economic world we all live in. Schools may seek to offer equality of opportunity, but without removing the barriers which some pupils encounter equality is likely to prove illusory.

Most of us accept that schools have a role in disciplining children, but the nature and extent of this role is debatable. In encouraging 'acceptable behaviour' schools may be creating a population which is unable to participate actively in the kinds of debates a true democracy needs. To what extent has socialisation merged into social control? Does this represent a threat to the ideals the UK holds dear?

The knowledge and experience gained in school help children acquire a sense of self and the society in which they live, how it has emerged, where it is at the moment and where it is going. If well done education has the potential to contribute to a society at ease with itself with a strong feeling of social cohesion. Badly done it is highly divisive. Despite many negative messages about the experience of schooling education also offers avenues of hope for the future. It does this because the potential for personal development and social transformation is always present. The message is clear: teachers and pupils together can change their understanding of the world and in so doing can transform both schooling and the wider society.

WHO ARE THE STUDENTS?

WHO'S IN EDUCATION IN THE UK?

WHO'S IN SCHOOL?

There are around 9.7 million pupils in school in the UK. They are mostly being educated in state-funded schools, but as Chapter 1 has shown provision is not uniform and pupils may go to school in a variety of different settings from the age of three until nineteen. Around 7 per cent are being educated privately, although these figures vary with a higher proportion of pupils in England than in Wales, Scotland or Northern Ireland.[1]

There is also nothing uniform about the pupils. They come from a variety of social backgrounds, and have different individual strengths and capabilities. Government statistics suggest that around 13.5 per cent come from families poor enough to warrant free school meals[2] and approximately 2.7 per cent have statements of special needs.[3] Twenty-two per cent of pupils are of minority ethnic origins with Asian pupils the largest group. In primary schools 15.2 per cent of pupils have a first language which is not English. Languages include Panjabi, Urdu, Bengali, Gujarati, Somali, Polish, Arabic, Portuguese and Turkish.[4]

There is also nothing uniform about pupils' experiences. Although mixed-sex schools are the norm, some attend single-sex schools and encounter the opposite sex only in their leisure time. Some pupils never meet children with an ethnicity different from their own. Others are used to a wide mix of peers from many different backgrounds. A good deal depends on what part of the UK they live in and, in larger conurbations, which area of the city. Some children with special needs are in special schools, but many are in mainstream schooling. Schools vary enormously in the experiences they offer pupils: some schools are very successful in getting good examination results; some inspire confidence through the care they offer children; some do both of these things and more, but there are others where children get a mostly negative experience. Children from affluent families frequently attend private schools with the advantage of small class sizes and considerable personal attention.

WHO'S IN UNIVERSITY?

Whilst the vast majority of children in the UK attend school, with up to 75 per cent staying on until age eighteen, those going on to higher education are still in a minority. At present the Higher Education Funding Council (HEFCE)[5] figures show that 36 per cent of eighteen year olds who live in England are in higher education. This has increased from around 30 per cent in the mid 1990s and 5 per cent in the 1960s. It still remains a considerably lower percentage than that of other European countries. However, as might be expected, there are considerable differences in participation rates according to gender, ethnicity and socio-economic background. Of late around 55 per cent of those in higher education have been female, with their male counterparts only accounting for 45 per cent of the total.

Despite government efforts to increase access to universities, children from the least advantaged areas of the UK are underrepresented, with one in five going on to HE as contrasted with one in two from more advantaged areas. Interestingly, in the most disadvantaged areas female participation in HE has increased whilst male participation has remained static. It has often been assumed that working class children choose not to go to university, but evidence suggests that, while steep rises in fees may deter some, others are prevented from entering because they have not achieved well enough in secondary education. The problem seems to lie with unequal access to good secondary schooling, rather than financial difficulties or problems of low aspiration.

The percentage of entrants to university of students from ethnic minority backgrounds in England has been steadily increasing and they now constitute 16 per cent of the student cohort. There are socio-economic differences within this group, however, and Pakistani and Bangladeshi students are the least likely to get into university with British Indians being the largest ethnic minority group in higher education. Ethnic minority students are concentrated in fewer universities than their white peers with over 20 per cent studying in London. This reflects the overall trend of ethnic minority students not moving away from home to attend university. Oxford and Cambridge recruit a far lower percentage of ethnic minority students than do other universities.[6]

The other important factor is that the more prestigious universities mentioned in Chapter 1 have tended to recruit from the public (i.e. private) schools rather than from the state sector. This is particularly so of Oxford and Cambridge. In Oxford University for example, despite strenuous efforts to increase diversity of intake, over 46 per cent of students still come from the independent sector.[7]

WHO IS DOING WELL AND WHO IS FAILING?

IN SCHOOL

This section has to be approached with caution since it is difficult to ascertain what 'doing well' really means. It has come to represent a narrow band of achievement in tests, but this omits a wide range of achievements which pupils rightly feel proud of. On the basis of test scores, the various countries in the UK measure performance differently. All publish the results of external examinations such as GCSE, but for younger children there are different ways of measuring attainment. In Scotland achievement is sampled with only a portion of pupils tested at any one time. The tests are anonymous and not related to individual schools or pupils. Different subjects are tested each year, so it is not possible as in other parts of the UK to give annual comparisons of the results of schools. Wales does look at annual achievement by schools in key subjects but this is based on teacher assessments rather than SATs, and Northern Ireland records GCSE results alone. In England, however, it is the results in the SATS tests of literacy and numeracy which measure success. SATS tests are taken annually by children aged seven and eleven which makes English pupils amongst the most tested in the world. In recent years there has been considerable controversy surrounding these tests. There were difficulties in marking the tests in 2009 and this led to a partial boycott in 2010 and an increased demand by some head teachers for their abolition.

ON THE INTERNATIONAL FRONT

In recent years pupil achievement has been subject to international analysis. The Programme for International Student Assessment (PISA), compares the achievements of fifteen-year-olds in reading, maths and science across the OECD countries. Finland has been top of the table in all three subjects in 2000, 2003 and 2006 respectively. The UK has slipped out of the top ten countries in recent years being ranked twenty-fourth in maths and seventeenth in literacy in the 2006 tests. Although having scored above average in the science tests a decline in performance in relation to this subject was also recorded in 2006. The reasons for different national performance are discussed in Chapter 7.

WHO ARE THE WINNERS AND LOSERS?

While acknowledging the difficulties relating to the statistics it is still possible to note differences in the way various groups of children perform: the winners and the losers. Over the past twenty years or so both girls' and boys' achievements has improved considerably, but girls are now consistently outperforming boys. Girls, both in the UK and abroad, have always done better in literacy, but they are now beginning to overtake boys in numeracy as well. Girls are doing particularly well at the higher SAT levels of achievement.[8] At the other end of the scale 80 per cent of those excluded from school are boys.[9] However when other variables are introduced such as ethnicity and social class a slightly different story emerges.

Pupils of Chinese origin do significantly better than all other groups, with Chinese girls having the best GCSE results. By contrast, the group with the worst GCSE results is African-Caribbean boys who are also among the poorest people in the UK and the most likely to be excluded from school. Whether you are poor or not is the strongest determinant of educational failure or success. Despite all the measured rises in achievement over the past decades, people from poorer backgrounds are still likely to do less well at school than their peers. A report published by the Sutton Trust in 2005 stressed that children born to poor families in the UK are less likely to achieve their full potential than similar children in other developed countries. Educational success in England, they concluded, is more related to wealth than in other similar countries.

At university level, women are doing better than men in that, overall, more are gaining upper second degrees.[10] They are also more likely to find jobs than their male counterparts after leaving university. However, the 'glass ceiling' still remains, and once in work men get promoted more easily than women and occupy more managerial positions. Male graduates still earn more money than their female colleagues. There is not a great deal of difference between the results obtained by white and ethnic minority students although African-Caribbean men are likely to do the least well at university. However, there is a big difference in job opportunities with all ethnic minority groups being considerably less likely to find graduate work than white graduates.

WHAT ARE THE REASONS FOR THESE DIFFERENCES?

BOYS AND GIRLS

Since the 1944 Education Act and the introduction of compulsory secondary education for all, there has been a focus on how boys and girls are doing in school. In the period 1950 to 1970 girls, with the exception of those in grammar schools, were underachieving. They did not have access to the full curriculum and were often required to study topics considered 'suitable' for girls such as domestic science. Many girls had limited aspirations and did not expect to have good jobs on leaving school. Even girls in private education had restricted views of potential careers. By the beginning of the twenty-first century much of this has changed. Girls are doing much better in school and interest is now focused on boys, particularly working class boys, who are doing less well although there has been some evidence recently that middle class boys are also underachieving.

BIOLOGICAL EXPLANATIONS FOR ACHIEVEMENT

In the early twentieth century there was a belief that differences in chromosome make-up, physiognomy and hormones explained the differences in achievement of both sexes. Whilst there is some evidence for biological differences between men and women these are difficult to assess. The problem was the belief that women were biologically inferior to men in every sense, mentally and physically. There were some tasks which were too difficult for women to understand or too physically demanding for them to do. The 1908 conference on infant mortality, for example, declared that too much education was bad for girls. It caused physiological damage even leading to sterility in women. These ideas cause amusement now, but it was doctors making these pronouncements then and they carried considerable force. Even in the 1940s suggestions were made that education for girls needed to be less mentally taxing with more opportunities given for them to focus on home life. Girls were therefore often marginalised in education, denied resources for their schooling and offered a restricted curriculum.

THE CONCEPT OF GENDER

Things began to change with the advent of feminist thinking in the 1960s and the understanding of the concept of gender. This has been touched on in Chapter 2 which showed that girls and boys learn what is expected of them through the process of socialisation. In any society children learn the appropriate behaviour for their sex. In the UK there is evidence that gender roles are changing: girls are doing well in school and university but the subtler gender messages in relation to work and employment still exist. Many girls in school are still not expecting to have good careers at the end of the day. The 2009 PISA report suggested that boys outperform girls in science to a far greater extent in the UK than elsewhere. In Turkey, for example, the girls did better than the boys and the report's authors suggested that gender stereotyping in the UK may be partly to blame for girls' poor achievement in science.

CHANGING ROLES

Ideas of what it means to be masculine in the UK today are also changing and may be contributing to boys' poorer performance at school. The last thirty years have seen a loss of male working class jobs, particularly those in heavy industry. This in turn has challenged traditional notions of masculinity. With the downturn in jobs generally boys are less able to see what they can aspire to and school increasingly appears irrelevant. There have been suggestions that this tendency is spreading to middle class-boys. Explanations have been offered for the trend. Given few challenges, with little demand being put upon them and a never-ending supply of parental support, there is nothing to make an effort for. Boys have lost their way, it seems. In many cultures the transition to manhood is a rite of passage and has been accompanied by tests and challenges. In modern societies no such rituals exist and boys are trapped in a never-ending cycle of adolescence. This has been fed it is claimed by a culture in the last thirty years which has suggested that huge sums of money can be acquired with little effort. For middle class boys it would be by making a killing in the City and for working class boys the chance of stardom through pop music or sport. Indeed the career service in schools has reported a large number of young children hoping for this kind of success.

THE SCHOOL EFFECT

Current ideas about masculinity and femininity affect the ways boys and girls perform at school, but the school itself also plays a part. There has been a growing trend in recent years towards primary and early-years teachers being women (see Chapter 5). There is now a widespread belief that the lack of male teachers in primary schools is having a detrimental effect on boys. Parents it seems, would like to see more men in classrooms and there have been attempts to involve fathers in both school and after-school activities. While recognising the importance of male role models generally some researchers have questioned whether more male teachers would actually reduce the gender gap in education. Bruce Carrington and others in an article entitled 'Role Models, school improvement and the gender gap' draws on a number of international studies which suggest that the sex of the teacher is not the key factor in relation to pupil achievement. From their own research Carrington *et al.* were able to draw similar conclusions. In fact they went on to say that female teachers were more likely to produce positive attitudes to learning in both boys and girls than were male teachers.

There have to be other explanations therefore for boys doing less well than girls. As Chapter 5 outlines teachers on the whole prefer conforming pupils, and these tend to be girls. Moreover, the structure of the current curriculum and the assessment methods may also favour girls. For example, girls do well in course work and less well in external exams. No explanation for how the different sexes perform is sufficient in its own right, however. Formal education interacts with the society it supports and the reasons for pupils' success or otherwise are complex.

PUPILS FROM MINORITY ETHNIC BACKGROUNDS

Individual identities do not relate solely to gender, powerful though this may be. Ethnic identity, whether it be UK white, Asian, African-Caribbean, Chinese or Polish, also plays a part. There are differences in the ways different ethnic groups perform. In the UK the debate has focused strongly around the low performance of African-Caribbean boys. In the United States similarly the spotlight has fallen on the dissimilar results of black and white students. What could be the reason for their relatively poor performance in school?

BIOLOGICAL EXPLANATIONS

As with gender, biological factors are sometimes used to explain ethnic differences, even though such explanations have been widely discredited. The Nobel Prize winner James Watson was interviewed by the *Sunday Times* in 2007.[11] In this interview he appeared to claim that race determines levels of intelligence. Black Africans, he suggested, had lower rates of intelligence than Europeans and white Americans. Intelligence, he maintained, is largely genetic and inherited and explains differences in achievement between black and white pupils. His claims follow in a long line of similar assertions which have been hotly disputed by the scientific community in general.

There are a number of problems with this explanation. Firstly, as has been shown in Chapter 1, there are disagreements about the concept of intelligence and how it is measured. In addition, in the past most intelligence tests have been culturally biased which means that they make most sense to people in the society for which they were devised. Secondly 'race' is a lazy term which has no scientific meaning. The so-called 'races' – caucasoid, negroid and mongoloid – were a crude eighteenth century means of classifying the peoples of the world. Biologists now agree that the categories are meaningless and that there are more differences *within* the groups than there are *between* them. The important thing is the way that people are perceived, and skin colour easily identifies people as different. 'Racial stereotyping' is the way society has taught people to have different assumptions about black and white people. It may be, then, that African-Caribbean pupils are not doing well in school not for biological reasons but because of prejudice, stereotyping and racism.

THE LEGACY OF HISTORY

The UK is a country made up of people from all over the world. Wave after wave of migrants have come to the UK for hundreds of years, had an impact on life here and contributed to the prosperity of the nation. Britain, however, has also been an imperial power. In the nineteenth century the British Empire dominated the world and the earliest school textbooks were proud to declare that over a quarter of the globe was coloured red and that the sun never set on the empire. With empire came belief in racial superiority. For George Gawler, the governor of South Australia in 1835, the native aborigines he encountered were uncivilised. The only hope for them was if they learnt to build houses, wear clothes and speak English. This was repeated throughout the empire. The British had come to civilise the masses.

RACIAL PREJUDICE

Although the world changed radically in the twentieth century, beliefs in racial superiority lingers on in the form of racial prejudice.

This was widespread after the war and still continues to this day. Prejudice is the pre-judging of people on the grounds of colour or perceived ethnicity. These judgements are usually negative and are frequently accompanied with stereotyping which is the process of making generalisations and then applying them to all members of a particular ethnic group. In school for example this might take the form of teachers thinking that African-Caribbean boys are good at sport but not at academic subjects. All pupils need teachers to have belief in their abilities; but African-Caribbean pupils, particularly boys, report that poor expectations on the part of teachers have had a depressing effect. There is more about this in Chapter 5.

RACISM

Prejudice becomes racism when those doing the disliking are in a position of power over those prejudiced against. *Personal* racism can vary from disrespect to harassment, violence and attacks. Anthony Walker for example, a black student from Merseyside was murdered in 2005 solely because of the colour of his skin. In addition to personal racism however there is a form of racism which can be termed *institutional* racism. This occurs when an organisation as a whole rather than an individual works to disadvantage minority groups. The murder of Stephen Lawrence in London in 1993 brought this idea to the fore. Stephen Lawrence was a sixth form student who was attacked by a gang of youths and murdered while he was waiting for a bus home. There were suggestions that the murder had a racist motive but although five suspects were arrested, no one was ever convicted. In 1999 Sir William Macpherson produced a report into Stephen Lawrence's death and identified what lessons could be learned from the affair. He stated that a considerable amount of personal racism had been detected in the attitudes of secondary, primary and even pre-school children but went on to suggest that institutional racism was also a problem. There had been failures in the police investigation which suggested that the organisation as a whole had not provided an appropriate service. The report did not suggest that all police personnel were racist but they identified structures and procedures within the police force which were detrimental to minority ethnic groups.

These findings led to a call for other public bodies to examine their own structures. In schools it raised questions as to the impact individual policies were having on ethnic minority students. The lack of ethnic minority teachers in positions of power, the nature of the National Curriculum and the number of black students permanently excluded from school raised the question of the degree of institutional racism which might be operating in schools and colleges. Macpherson recommended that the National Curriculum should be amended to prevent racism and to reflect the diverse society the UK now is. He also argued that schools should implement strategies to deal with racism and that all racist incidents in school should be recorded and publicly reported. School inspections should establish how well these strategies were being implemented.

WHAT HAS BEEN DONE TO REMEDY THE SITUATION?

Awareness and change of attitude in relation to ethnic minority groups have occurred, but it has been slow and patchy. The post-war aim of schooling for ethnic minorities, known as 'immigrant education', was to assimilate all pupils into the dominant culture. This policy was not unlike the old civilising of the natives. Black pupils were expected to 'fit in' with the prevailing culture and an emphasis was placed on English Language teaching. The injustice of this approach eventually was recognised and initiatives to deal with racism and ethnicity were taken. In 1976 the Labour government introduced the Race Relations Act which prohibited discrimination against anyone on racial grounds. This Act applied to schools and rendered it illegal to refuse admission on the grounds of race or to not offer all pupils the benefits, facilities or services available. It laid the basis for what was to follow.

MULTICULTURAL EDUCATION

The Swann Report in 1985 testified that African-Caribbean children were underachieving in school and categorically denied that this had anything to do with intelligence: underachievement was strongly linked to poverty and prejudice. The report stated that ethnic minorities should be able to keep their own languages and maintain their own cultural heritage. It also highlighted the need to tackle racism in schools. It was not a question of how to educate black pupils; rather there should be a strong commitment to 'education for all'. It recommended that multi-cultural education be introduced in schools and promoted at a national level, rather than being left to local authorities. In school this led to attempts to celebrate different cultures emphasising the positive aspects of cultural diversity.

ANTI-RACIST EDUCATION

Multicultural approaches, however, did little to tackle the levels of racism and in some areas anti-racist education supplemented or replaced it. Schools, it was thought, needed a policy on race where complaints about racism could be heard and dealt with. Further, schools themselves should teach about racism. School structures and practices should be systematically examined and a curriculum should be created which was liberating and transformative. These developments occurred during the 1980s and 1990s but progress was slow. Governments did not prioritise them and the prospect of change was not helped by some teachers who sought to minimise the significance of race which they found a difficult and sensitive issue to deal with. This was particularly true in all-white schools. 'No problem here' was a typical response from such schools, but in fact quite the reverse was true. The problem was very definitely in their court. 'Education for all' meant tackling the beliefs of the dominant white groups in single culture schools.

Following MacPherson's report the government brought in the Race Relations (Amendment) Act 2000 which recognised institutional racism and required all organisations and employers to have a policy for race equality. The setting up of faith schools allowed some pupils to escape in-school prejudice, but this has also led to further segregation. Things have been slow to change and racism and prejudice still contribute substantially to the failure of some students of ethnic minority origins.

PUPILS FROM DIFFERENT SOCIAL CLASSES

Despite class being difficult to measure and there being evidence that it has changed form in recent years, it is still a major determinant of educational achievements.

WORKING CLASS CHILDREN AND UNDERACHIEVEMENT

It is easy to see how education could give advantage to the upper classes but why are working class children doing comparatively badly in state education compared with middle class children of similar ability? Post-war educationalists thought that material environment and poor nutrition might have an effect on how well children did in school. Children who were inadequately fed and lacked material comforts would be unable to perform well. A famous study by J. W. B. Douglas, *The Home and the School*, published in 1964 found nutrition to be less important than had been imagined. Douglas found that between the ages of eight and eleven children's performance in tests was greatly influenced by both home and school. The pupil's capacity to improve depended on parental attitudes and also on the academic record of the school itself. Overall unsatisfactory material conditions were only thought to have a minor effect on the pupil's performance. This was reinforced by the Plowden Report in 1967 which suggested that parental attitudes and maternal care were more important than the level of material needs.

Some credence has been given in recent years to the idea that material factors and nutrition do play a part in underachievement as links between nutrition and performance have been demonstrated. The New Labour government instituted 'breakfast clubs' in part to rectify these problems. The clubs were to help ensure that pupils regularly eat a healthy breakfast before starting their school day. Jamie Oliver's campaign to improve school dinners addresses the same concerns.

CLASS ATTITUDES AND VALUES

Values and attitudes also play a part. A wave of research in the 1960s attempted to show that working class attitudes were not competitive enough. They were based on solidarity and did not encourage children to compete in the same way as their middle class peers. The research was obviously assuming that competition is better than co-operation. Competition may indeed be an appropriate aspect of schooling but it has dominated schooling in the last twenty years in particular, pitching pupil against pupil and school against school. Might more co-operation be beneficial, and how might the classroom and teaching methods, reflect this?

LANGUAGE ACQUISITION

Bernstein writing in 1975 suggested that the type of socialisation a child received affected his/her speech and had profound effects on educational achievement. He identified different codes of speech which he labelled 'restricted' and 'elaborated'. Children using restricted codes were able to communicate with only a limited number of people, namely those with whom the child shared the same assumptions and meanings. Elaborated codes, on the other hand, are context-free and allow children to function in many different situations. Elaborated codes are the ones used in school. Bernstein did not link his codes directly to class but his research fixed in people's minds the idea that working class was in some ways inadequate.

CULTURAL DEPRIVATION

This theory suggests that working class children have been brought up with negative attitudes to schooling with parents uninterested in formal education. These children are thought to lack role models with few in their family who had experienced post-sixteen or university education. Their tastes and knowledge were far removed from that of the school. Children born to the lower classes would therefore need 'compensatory' education.

SCHOOL AND WORKING CLASS CHILDREN

It is not just parental background which is related to underachievement. The school has its part to play and education has a record of not meeting the needs of working class children. The way schooling is organised is a major contributor to this. In the early days of comprehensive education pupils in secondary schools were 'streamed', that is, divided up into separate classes according to ability. There was not much movement between streams, and where pupils started at eleven was where they were likely to end up at sixteen. The lower streams were largely where working class children were to be found. Later schools changed to a banding system; most schools had two bands with perhaps a remedial addition. The bands roughly divided the children between those thought likely to succeed academically (band A) and those thought likely not to (band B). The working class children mostly ended up in band B and there they stayed. Moreover, teachers often had expectations about the likely performance and behaviour of working class children which were mostly detrimental. This is discussed further in Chapter 5.

SCHOOL AND MIDDLE CLASS CHILDREN

On the whole middle class children do well at school but why is this? Pierre Bourdieu identified patterns of class domination in education. The middle class possess what is known as 'cultural capital'. This is the knowledge and experience which allow them to influence events. They know how to manipulate the system to get the results they need and he maintained that they use this to gain educational advantage. Far from offering equal opportunity the education system in Western societies, he suggests, is the conduit through which power and privilege are transferred from one generation to the next. Stephen Ball drawing on more recent evidence supports this thesis (see the section on parental choice in Chapter 1). The middle class have the skills of 'assertive talk' and enough cultural capital to ensure the success of their children. The pupils themselves understand the language of the school and often have aspirations which match those of the schools. In the main they have an expectation that they will be successful at school and this belief is frequently supported by their teachers. At home they are likely to have their own personal space equipped with a computer. Stephen Ball argued in 2008 that the class divide in education is now as stark as it was in Victorian times.

POVERTY

Gender, ethnicity and class are all important in determining success or otherwise at school but by far the key predictor of school success is the degree of relative poverty. Poverty is related to social class. In the last decade the number of children deemed to be living in poverty has decreased, but the UK's record of eliminating poverty is still poor. In 1997 it was ranked fifteenth out of fifteen EU countries. In 2005 it came eleventh but was still below Italy, Spain and Portugal. More important, the gap between the rich and poor in the UK has widened remarkably in the last thirty years.[12] This widening began in the 1980s under the Conservative government and was barely held constant under the subsequent New Labour Governments.

Why does this gap matter? Richard Wilkinson and Kate Pickett in their book *The Spirit Level* have demonstrated that it is not the absolute level of wealth or poverty in any one country that matters; it is the size of the gap between the rich and the poor that makes the difference. In countries which are more equal people are almost always more healthy, have longer life expectancies, have better educational outcomes and lower levels of imprisonment and punishment. And this does not just apply to the poorer end of society: surprisingly, in more equal societies the rich also benefit with improved health and better educational results. In common parlance more equality is a win–win situation. The converse is that more unequal societies have worse results on all indices.

The question must immediately be asked, where does the UK stand in the international tables of inequality and the answer is, near the bottom. In Europe only Portugal is lower, and in the world generally the United States and Singapore are worse. Japan and Finland are at the top of the table even though they have very different societies and political systems. The research conclusions are very powerful: in order to improve educational outcomes the UK needs to address and rectify its gross income inequalities.

ATTEMPTS TO DEAL WITH WORKING CLASS UNDERACHIEVEMENT: SURE START AND ECM

From the introduction of secondary education for all to the period when comprehensive schools were introduced, successive Labour governments attempted to deal with working class underachievement with little success. From the year 2000 the government began to realise that children from low socio-economic backgrounds were falling behind from birth and that early intervention was necessary on a number of fronts. Every Child Matters, the Sure Start programme in England, and Cymorth Cymru in Wales have aimed to remedy the situation by providing a unified approach. It was recognised that the problems the young children and their families face could not be adequately dealt with by separate professionals working in isolation from each other. A joined-up approach involving health, education and family support was implemented. Initial evaluations suggest that there has been some success with children and parents both reporting that integrated services have made a difference. There are difficulties, however. Professionals who work in totally different ways have found it difficult to come together and in the long run, while the aims of the policies are undoubtedly good, the reality may not measure up to them.

SPECIAL-NEEDS PUPILS

Despite the difficulties encountered at different times by groups who have been educationally disadvantaged, there remains one group who have on occasions been denied any education at all. It is those deemed to have special educational needs. This includes children with physical or mental disabilities as well as those with emotional and behavioural difficulties. It ranges from children with acute physical disabilities to ones with mild dyslexia. In reality there is little that unites this group of children except their exclusion or marginalisation in the education system.

For much of the late nineteenth and early twentieth centuries attention was focused on the children's disabilities rather than the child as a whole or on the environment in which she/he was growing up. 'Idiot', 'feebleminded' or even 'moral defective' were terms used to describe special-needs children at this time. They were thought to be unteachable and were largely hidden from view. They were frequently taken from their parents and brought up in institutions. Many recounted their feelings of separation and unworthiness. Very few received the education they warranted.

CHANGES WHICH HAVE OCCURRED

The 1944 Education Act decreed that all children were educable and special-needs children were reclassified as 'subnormal' or 'remedial'; but these terms were little better than the previous ones. Being subnormal suggests that the person is not quite human, and indeed it has been the labelling of pupils in this way which has been part of the problem. It was a tragedy for many who, while having some disability, were as bright, intelligent and educable as the rest. Many children at this time were placed in special schools. The problem revolved around identifying the disability and finding a cure for it if possible or trying to reduce its effects. Disability was seen as a medical condition, equated with chronic illness with all the attendant problems that such labelling brought.

THE 1981 EDUCATION ACT

As time went by society's attitude changed and a different understanding of disability emerged which put emphasis on the social barriers to a good life that disabled people face. Perhaps it was society and the education system that were the problem rather than the pupils themselves. Society was putting up barriers rather than helping children attain their true potential. These barriers ranged from buildings which couldn't take wheelchairs through to repressive social attitudes which made disabled children unacceptable. A major contribution to the change in attitude came as a result of the Warnock Report of 1978. The terminology altered and 'learning difficulties' replaced the former vocabulary. The emphasis was modified from looking at a pupil's *condition* to looking at his or her *needs*. In the 1981 Act which followed this, children went through a succession of assessments which might eventually lead to a statement. The statement indicated that a child needed additional support. Children, wherever possible, would be educated in mainstream schools which would need to adapt their buildings and teaching and learning strategies accordingly. In recent times a more 'affirmative' approach to disability has gradually been adopted. Disabled athletes have led the way in demonstrating what young people, often with considerable physical disabilities, can achieve. Nevertheless progress is slow and the media in 2010 focused on a number of tragic cases in which disabled youngsters had been bullied and abused, often by their peers.

INCLUSIVE EDUCATION

Current educational policies focus on the notion of 'inclusion'. Although the 1980s saw more and more children educated in main stream schooling, they were often 'integrated' rather than 'included'.

So they might attend the same school as their peers but be educated in separate classes and in reality lead separate lives. This, it was argued, contravenes a child's human rights. Inclusion means being in the same classroom as the others, being offered the same curriculum and being treated in a way which makes the pupil feel no different from the others.

Despite the Labour government's encouragement, progress towards inclusion has been slow. Firstly, there were worries from teachers who did not feel sufficiently trained to teach special-needs children. In reality what has happened is that it is teaching assistants who support children in class; but this raises questions as to whether it is the best arrangement for the pupils themselves or whether they would benefit from more specialist teaching outside the classroom. Secondly, resources were needed to accompany such changes and these were often not forthcoming or slow in arriving. Thirdly, the emphasis in recent years on a competitive, test-driven culture in schools has affected all pupils. It is very difficult to celebrate diversity in a schooling system which is not child-centred and which measures its success in terms of performance in standard tests.

WHAT DOES IT MEAN TO BE A PUPIL?

It would be wrong to leave this discussion on students without considering what it really means to be a pupil. We have all been pupils. Most of us have strong recollections of schooling but these are only memories filtered and changed by time. What does research tell us about being a pupil and, perhaps more important, what do young people themselves say about their experience?

RESEARCHERS' VIEWS

Researchers were initially more interested in what education did in general: who was receiving the education and did it change life chances? Slowly, though, they began to realise that what was going on in classrooms was of prime importance in understanding what education was about and they began to focus on seeing things from the pupil's point of view. Many of the accounts by educationalists have been from their own personal observations and from their interviews with students.

LIFE IN PRIMARY SCHOOLS IN THE 1960S

P. W. Jackson, writing at the end of the 1960s, drew a particularly bleak view of the US school where he said the child was a virtual prisoner. Going to school for the first time is not an easy process, he maintained. Children had to move from their families which are usually small and personal to an institutional setting which is largely impersonal. In so doing they had to deal with three fundamental aspects of institutional life. Firstly, they had to learn to be alone in a crowded situation: schools, he suggested, created a degree of anonymity. There are large numbers of people and children move from being special at home to being one of a crowd at school. Secondly, they have to deal with continual evaluation. Life at school is very competitive and pupils are being constantly measured against each other, judged and often found lacking. Finally, pupils have to learn to deal with unequal and, to a degree, impersonal relationships.

LIFE IN MODERN PRIMARY SCHOOLS

Jackson was writing more than forty years ago about US inner city schools. Surely this can have little relevance for primary schools in the UK at the beginning of the twenty-first century? Primary schools have certainly changed and relationships have become far less impersonal. They may look like warm, welcoming places, and indeed many are; but closer scrutiny undermines this general view. Children know all too well that classrooms are places where they are tested, measured and divided up according to their perceived abilities. Fifty years ago this might have been all too obvious. Older people have memories today of having been tested weekly and on Monday morning placed in class order where they would remain for the rest of the week. It was dreadful to be permanently at the bottom of the class, but children in the top group also suffered anxiety lest they slip a place and move down a seat.

Of course this doesn't happen in primary schools today, or does it? In many primary schools children are divided into groups, often based on their perceived ability in English and maths, and these groups rarely interact with each other. Follow the children into the playground and they are often playing with their peers from the same group. Children understand the grouping system very well and, despite all attempts by teachers to hide the differences between groups, the pupils are well aware of what these are. The author's daughter aged five came proudly home after two days in school to declare she was in the red group. It was obvious to the little girl that red was good and that to have been in the green group would have been disastrous.

Schools can indeed be lonely places and sometimes can feel overbearing. Asked to draw pictures of themselves at home and at school, many young children draw themselves large at home and colour themselves brightly. By contrast more pictures of school are in black and white and often show very little people sitting at very large desks. Testing and evaluation appear to be increasing year on year in English schools. There are checklists which indicate what three-year-olds should be achieving, and in England children are tested as early as age seven. Evaluation is the order of the day. Jackson concluded that although few people totally disliked school, few were totally positive about the experience. Similar mixed feelings are currently documented in the UK. The views of pupils themselves are recorded below. It is worth noting however that *The Cambridge Primary Review* edited by Robin Alexander reporting in 2009 while offering major criticisms of primary education in England, found that schools were on the whole doing well under pressure and highly valued by parents and pupils.

LIFE IN SECONDARY SCHOOLS

Jackson was writing about primary schools, but what of secondary schools? Pupils are more institutionalised on entering secondary school and therefore perhaps more accepting of the classroom reality. Paul Willis, writing in the 1970s about boys in an English secondary modern school, suggested that pupils had indeed adapted to classroom life. He put forward the view that in this instance they were consumed by boredom and had found ways to cope with the tedium by 'having a laugh', harassing the teachers and on occasions resorting to lunchtime drinking. They also mocked the school by wearing their uniforms in an inappropriate way. The last resort was truancy. Looking at some secondary schools today there is evidence of all these adaptations. Many young teachers struggle to keep order in the face of harassment. Pupils as a whole frequently adapt their clothing to stress their individuality and to mock the institutional effects of school life, and there is still selective truancy.

Research in the 1980s suggested that while some pupils support the aims of the school, others engage in a kind of guerrilla warfare to undermine its control. There has been a good deal of debate, however, as to the strength or success of such resistance. Boys, mostly at that time working class, who defied school norms often ended up with few qualifications and a lifetime of poorly paid jobs or unemployment. These trends have endured and show little indication of lessening.

PUPILS IN THEIR OWN WORDS

But what have pupils themselves got to say? What does it mean to be a pupil and what can politicians and educationalists learn from what pupils can tell them? In the UK we have been slow to elicit pupils' views. This may relate to a long tradition which has generally thought of children as immature and unable to give a rational judgement about their own best needs. This has changed in the last ten years when there has been an unprecedented national and international focus on consulting pupils and with hearing the pupil voice. Over and over again pupils understand what the problems are and offer credible solutions. The responses in Burke and Grosvenor's book suggest that, despite the endless 'improvements' in schooling, children in 2001 reflected the same concerns as their predecessors did in 1969. Being a pupil involves being talked at and not listened to. It entails having no voice in one's own education and no representation. Above all it means being passive. Schooling is by and large only there to be endured but the mitigating factor as always was that schooling allowed pupils to make friends and to have daily contact with them.

CONCLUSION

The children most likely to succeed in current schooling are the sons and daughters of the middle classes, although there is evidence to suggest that success may be beginning to elude some middle class boys. They do well because their parents have ensured that they attend state schools with the best academic results, they speak the language of the school and are supported by teachers who on the whole expect them to be successful. The children most likely to fail come from the poorest backgrounds. They experience lives where a large number of elements combine to produce hurdles which only a few can overcome, notably inadequate parental income, poor living conditions and low expectations. In addition for some there is the added problem of racism. Some pupils enjoy school, but many, while getting pleasure from meeting their friends, despair of their inability to have a say in how schools are run or what can be done to improve their lot.

4

WHAT ARE WE TEACHING STUDENTS IN SCHOOLS AND UNIVERSITIES AND WHY?

WHAT ARE WE TEACHING PUPILS IN SCHOOL?

Most people, remembering their own schooldays would say that schools are teaching essential knowledge which represents a clear and objective way of looking at the world. Knowledge is divided into subjects or topics depending on the pupils' age and is known as 'the curriculum'. The subjects are said to represent the best selection of knowledge available. It is knowledge worth having, and is selected by experts for the benefit of students, even if the benefit is not obvious to students themselves. Some subjects are thought to be essential, even if there is disagreement about the relative importance of others. For example, everyone needs to read, write and add up, therefore English and maths must be central to the primary school curriculum.

HOW RELIABLE ARE THESE COMMONSENSE VIEWS?

Is the curriculum sensible and objective? We have all spent hours in school and we come to accept knowledge when it is selected, organised, disseminated and reinforced by others. This experience is even stronger when a national curriculum makes all pupils in the country study the same things, often at the same times. The curriculum comes to be seen as inevitable: proscribed, and beyond debate. The only problem is an organisational one: how to cover all the subjects in the time allowed.

In fact the curriculum is contentious, potentially explosive and subject in many countries to close political scrutiny. What is taught in schools and universities really matters because it structures what we know and influences our beliefs and values. It helps make us who we are. So it is imperative to stand back from experience and from taken-for-granted beliefs and to look again at what is actually being taught in schools. Is it the right kind of knowledge? Is it organised in a suitable way? Who should have access to it, and above all who should decide what the curriculum should contain?

THE CURRICULUM: A DEFINITION

Basically, the curriculum is the sum of the knowledge pupils are exposed to in a formal schooling setting. This is not a fixed entity. It is a selection from all available knowledge and the organisation of this into a more or less coherent whole. The amount of knowledge in the world is enormous and increasing at an exponential rate; so the decision about what to include becomes quite a test. The task is analogous with having a five minute dash around the supermarket to pick up your prize of a trolleyful of goodies. It is likely to be a very partial selection. This is the scale of the challenge. It is surely, however, not such a random snatch. There must be defining principles and recognised ways of organising the curriculum which can be applied to the selection of material. Indeed there are and they are discussed later in the chapter. Beyond just content, however, the curriculum is intimately connected with learning, teaching and assessment. The ways in which knowledge is conceived and organised affects the way pupils learn. The teacher's understanding of the curriculum and the demands of assessment affect the content and how it is taught. These issues are discussed further in Chapter 5.

In the end the curriculum reflects particular views of knowledge and learning and is a public statement of what constitutes official and 'real' knowledge. The history of the curriculum in England and Wales for the first 100 years of compulsory education has been one of debate as to which pupils should have access to which areas of urriculum. In the last thirty years the arguments have centred on who should decide what the content of the curriculum should be.

SCHOOL KNOWLEDGE

WHERE DID SCHOOL KNOWLEDGE COME FROM?

In school we encounter recognized bodies of knowledge in the form of subjects or 'disciplines'. Even though methods of teaching may have changed, many of the subjects in the curriculum were well known to our parents and grandparents, but where did this knowledge come from? Western education is largely the product of the Enlightenment. This was the European movement which over the past 400 years has had a profound effect on what we believe and think. It turned the world upside down by questioning the validity of traditional knowledge which had tended to rest on the authority of religion.

For Enlightenment thinkers the universe was rational and could best be understood by the application of reason. Claims for truth should be open to questioning and able to be verified. Enlightenment thinkers also believed that human beings could be improved through being educated and national education systems were created in part to propagate these ideas. There was, therefore, a stress on the importance of fostering cognitive (thinking) skills. In the school curriculum a strong emphasis was placed on science and maths which has lasted to this day when the world has come to rely more and more on these subjects. The highest French baccalaureate, for example, is the one in mathematics.

WHAT COUNTS AS KNOWLEDGE?

We tend to think of knowledge as fixed and absolute but this is frequently far from the truth. Peter Berger and Thomas Luckmann in *The Social Construction of Reality* suggested that humans create knowledge and then experience it as something other than their creation. People interact with each other and come to a shared understanding of how the world is. This understanding is transferred to the next generation and 'hardens' in the process so that the subsequent cohort receives the knowledge as absolute when in reality it is much more contentious. We tend to think of scientific knowledge in particular as being beyond debate but over time many findings become disputed and what was taken as absolute at the point of discovery is later called into question.

In modern times we have tended to see scientific explanations as having more validity than other forms of knowledge. This view has been associated with a rise in scientism which holds the belief that science is the only route to 'real' knowledge. This has been contested by Russell Stannard,[1] a physics professor who while accepting the importance of scientific discoveries has disputed that science can provide answers to everything. Scientism has brought science into competition with religion but the subjects have different aims. Confusion arises when they are seen as serving the same purpose.

Distinctions have been made between *propositional* knowledge which is 'the knowing' of facts and *procedural* knowledge which can best be described as know-how. In education this has often led to a separation between 'academic' and 'practical' subjects. The British education system has always prized the former. In northern European countries, including Germany, however, there is a strong belief that knowledge must start with the way in which individuals function in the 'real' world. Learning manual trades in school is as important as intellectual activities. In the Danish system textile design, woodwork and home economics are compulsory.

The problem with school knowledge is that it becomes self-validating as *official* knowledge so that other forms of knowledge become of lesser importance. There are often examples of children bringing stories from their home lives which are disparaged by the teacher. In a similar way the oral traditions which have historically been so important for conveying truths of various kinds have largely been neglected in favour of tidier better formulated and packaged knowledge. First World or indigenous peoples such as Australian Aborigines, Native Americans or Arctic Inuit have a very different way of understanding the world and this is considered in Chapter 7. Western schooling has tended to exclude this, but in so doing has it cut out an important part of the human experience?

WHAT SUBJECTS SHOULD BE TAUGHT IN SCHOOL?

There is considerable agreement in Western societies about what should be taught in school, even if there are different ways of teaching it. Literacy, numeracy, and scientific skills are still of extreme importance. Beyond this, however, there are major areas of disagreement. Should the arts be taught in school? In true Enlightenment tradition, the French curriculum has tended to marginalise creative subjects, regarding them as leisure activities. The Scandinavian countries have often prioritised them.

Predictably, one of the main areas of conflict is the teaching of religious education. The Church in England has had a major impact on the school curriculum, and in Norway Christian religious education is an essential part of a child's education. Others countries take a completely different view. After the revolution, France declared itself a secular society and religious education was banned from the curriculum. There may be some discussion on the relative contributions of religious beliefs as part of ethics and philosophy, but religion is considered to be personal and the responsibility of the family. France has strongly resisted attempts by any organised religion to influence the curriculum.

A similar situation pertains in the United States, although for different reasons. Religion is not taught in schools and this might seem strange since the United States sees itself as a strongly religious country. Early in its history, however, different religious groups were engaged in strife and discrimination. Thomas Jefferson, the third US President, thought it was important to build 'a wall of separation between the Church and the State'. Religious teaching was to be excluded from state schools and parents wanting religious education were required to pay for private education. The issue was taken further in the 1960s when the federal government decided that prayer should be removed from state schools. This caused annoyance amongst Christians and, with the rise of right-wing fundamentalism in the United States, there have been attempts to bring religion back into the classroom.

SUBJECT CONTENT

As well as debate about which subjects should be taught, there is debate about the content of the subjects. Through the teaching of history, literature and religion, pupils gain a sense of national identity and these subjects have a profound effect on pupils' understanding of the world they live in: not only who they are but also where they came from. It is not surprising that in democratic societies controversy surrounds these subjects. The teaching of history in the UK is a good example.

History can be taught in a variety of ways. Traditionally it has been taught chronologically, from the Norman Conquest to World War II. Recently, a more piecemeal approach had been adopted with the emphasis on process: how you *do* history, rather than what history tells us. There are legitimate arguments for both approaches. When the Conservative government brought in the National Curriculum in 1988 they favoured a chronological approach to the teaching of history. They also wanted a version of history which would have a single agreed narrative focusing on the 'ancient British people'. Objections were raised to this: Britain was a country which was diverse and multicultural. It didn't have a single agreed narrative and many people had no connection with ancient British people. The Conservatives were in government and so their version of history prevailed. The history curriculum was changed again when New Labour came to power in 1997 and is set for further change since the general election of 2010.

IDEOLOGICAL MESSAGES

History may seem an obvious subject for controversy, but no subjects are neutral. All subjects in the curriculum are underpinned by beliefs, values and ideological messages. Values are obviously important because without them children would lack any form of moral guidance; but in a democratic society we need to be absolutely clear which values are being promoted. In a loosely framed national curriculum a whole variety of values might exist but in a tightly organised curriculum the values underlying the selection of knowledge become very important.

Maths may seem to be the most neutral of subjects, but examples taken from different countries suggest that this is not the case and maths problems frequently reflect the ideological outlook of the country concerned. Clive Harber, in his article on political education, cites a number of examples where mathematics is used to make an ideological point. One example taken from Richard Dawson's work *Political Socialization* shows how Cuba set maths questions which asked pupils to calculate how many times per month the United States violated Cuban air space. In this case in studying maths pupils were learning political messages. It is easy to dismiss the Cuban approach as indoctrination, but maths in Britain also contains social messages. Dawson also cites the work of Maxwell who in his dissertation 'Is Mathematics Education Politically Neutral?' looked at the mathematics topics in use in schools. They were to do with mortgages, investment and interest suggesting that these issues were of central importance for most people. There was little on how to live on social security payments. Feminists have also pointed out that many of the examples used in maths involved men. Women were marginalised and when portrayed at all were usually in a subservient role. All these seem minor examples, but cumulatively they give a strong ideological message.

WHAT IS LEFT OUT?

Perhaps just as important as what is in a curriculum is what is left out. For years the UK taught little of the slave trade and the degree to which Britain's wealth depended upon it. It would be wrong to suggest that the English are the sole users of history in this way. Most countries have done similar things. Japan has removed from its history curriculum any reference to the Nanjing massacre of July 1937 in which numerous Chinese people including many women were brutally murdered by Japanese soldiers.

Subjects are often taught using textbooks. These books appear authoritative. We tend to believe what we read in such books, but is the knowledge reliable? Michael Apple in his book *Educating the Right Way* illustrates numerous ways in which right-wing activists have put pressure on textbook publishers in the United States. Textbook writers producing books for use in junior and senior high schools in the state of Texas for example were instructed to stress patriotism, obedience to authority and discouragement of 'deviance'. Texas is a big state and amongst the biggest purchaser of textbooks so it is in a position to dictate content. Other states later bought the books. Apple also noted the editing of content. For example, Martin Luther King's famous 'I have a dream' speech was only included in textbooks when his references to the extreme racism blacks had experienced were removed.

DIFFERENT WAYS OF ORGANISING KNOWLEDGE: SUBJECTS

Until now the discussion has been around subjects and their content. Learning through subjects is the way we are most familiar with; but how valid is this as a way of organising knowledge? Paul Hirst in 1975 argued that it is very valid indeed. He maintained that there are universal forms of knowledge which he divided into seven areas, namely mathematics, physical sciences, human sciences, history, religion, literature and the fine arts, philosophy and moral knowledge. Each of these subject areas is discrete and has its own content and methods of study. To be knowledgeable pupils need to be taught the relevant information and methods of study which are pertinent for each area of knowledge. The curriculum should, therefore, follow the established forms of knowledge and children should be taught in traditional subject format. To be an educated person, he maintained, one needed access to all these knowledge areas.

DIFFERENT WAYS OF ORGANISING KNOWLEDGE: TOPICS AND INTEGRATION

Whilst not necessarily disagreeing with the notion that there are discrete forms of knowledge, others have maintained that teaching pupils through separate subjects is not the best way to foster understanding. Children see the world as a whole and dividing it up into subject areas disrupts this totality of experience and presents the world in an unnecessarily fragmented form. Teachers, it is argued, may well understand how subjects are organised and developed, but this information is rarely conveyed to children. This thinking led to projects on curriculum integration in the 1970s and teaching through topics. In topic teaching the teacher might select a theme such as 'water' and the class would learn about this from a variety of standpoints. The pupils might look at water from a scientific, historical or geographical viewpoint, but they might also write a poem or paint a picture thus offering a more holistic view of the topic. This approach fits well with the constructivist views of learning outlined in Chapter 5.

In more recent times, at all levels of education from schools to universities, stress has been placed on the practical application of knowledge. This suggests that knowledge is most useful when applied to the solving of problems. Education, therefore, might begin with a problem and then use a cross-curricular approach, bringing to bear a number of disciplines in its solution. Critics have pointed out that knowledge of basic subject matter is needed before this approach can be utilised.

WHO SHOULD HAVE ACCESS TO THE CURRICULUM?

In modern times a typical response might be that of course everyone is equally entitled to have access to all knowledge. In the past, however, depending on class, gender, ethnicity and measured intelligence, pupils in England and Wales have had differing access to the curriculum. The history of the curriculum in England and Wales during much of the twentieth century has been the history of the fight for equal access for all.

1870S: ONE CURRICULUM FOR THE RICH AND ANOTHER FOR THE POOR

The Taunton Report of 1868 suggested that the curriculum should be developed to cover three grades of pupil. The grades reflected social class. First grade pupils who were expected to stay in school until aged eighteen and not expected to work for a living would receive a classical education. Second grade pupils, leaving at age sixteen, might study some Latin but only if this did not interfere with the learning of subjects which would be practical for a life in business. Pupils in the third grade could not be expected to stay on in school beyond the age of fourteen and were likely to end up doing manual work. They would be taught the basic skills of reading, writing and arithmetic. From the beginning of formal education for all there was a clear class divide in the provision. Academic subjects were prized more highly than vocational ones. These two factors have characterised the English education system ever since.

Third-graders were also to be instilled with a particular kind of religion. It was a religion which supported the class system and made it clear that a person's position in life was God-given. Hymns like 'All things bright and beautiful' were regularly sung in state schools and included the verse 'The rich man in his castle, the poor man at his gate, God made them high and lowly and ordered their estate'. This hymn is still around today, although that verse is not heard. At the end of the nineteenth century class differences and educational opportunities were ordained by God, and therefore sacrosanct.

POST-WORLD WAR II: DIVISIONS CONTINUE

After World War II the 1944 Education Act established secondary education for all up to the age of fifteen. This seemed a major step forward, but the selective tripartite system with grammar, technical and secondary modern schools offered children a very different curriculum depending on which type of school they went to. Children in grammar schools followed a traditional academic education based on separate sciences and some modern and classical languages. The vast majority of children in secondary modern schools studied a curriculum which was considered 'practical' and would lead directly to apprenticeships or employment. Although the eleven-plus exam allowed some working class pupils, to attend grammar schools, these institutions tended to draw pupils mainly from middle class homes. Class still ruled in schooling and academic subjects were still more highly prized than practical ones.

COMPREHENSIVE EDUCATION AND ACCESS FOR ALL

With the widespread introduction of comprehensive schools in the 1970s access to the curriculum changed. The raising of the school leaving age in 1972 to sixteen meant that many more children were taking examinations. The replacement of the GCE Ordinary Level and the Certificate of Secondary Education (CSE) which had been recently introduced into secondary modern schools with the new General Certificate of Secondary Education (GCSE) opened up access to the curriculum to a much wider group of pupils. Most comprehensive schools taught a watered-down version of the grammar school curriculum and although practical and vocational skills became more prominent they were definitely second best compared with academic skills. The hoped-for development of a more exciting and innovative curriculum did not take place and an opportunity for change was perhaps wasted.

A CORE CURRICULUM

BACKGROUND TO THE DEBATE IN ENGLAND

Until the 1980s what should be taught in school was largely decided by schools and local education authorities, although at the later stages of schooling national exam boards influenced curriculum content. As the 1970s progressed, with increasing economic decline and social disorder, the spotlight was turned on schools. Perhaps schools were in some way not producing the skills needed for an advanced industrial nation. In 1973 Anthony Crosland, Labour Minister of Education, complained that the school curriculum was 'a secret garden in which only teachers and children are allowed to walk' and the speech caught the mood of the times. In 1976 James Callaghan, the Labour Prime Minister, opened the 'great debate' on the role of schooling in the second half of the twentieth century and this was to propel education into the national spotlight. Perhaps there was a need for a national approach to what was taught in schools. It led to a debate on the necessity of having a core curriculum

THE CASE FOR A CORE CURRICULUM

Many countries in the world including European countries operate a core curriculum, and a strong case can be made for this. Firstly it can be argued that a country needs to agree what the aims of its education system are, and then to realise them through a national curriculum. Secondly, a specified core curriculum would give opportunity for all to succeed. Reviews of the English primary curriculum in the early 1980s had demonstrated that there was very unequal access to basic subjects such as mathematics and science. A core curriculum would indicate what should be taught at each stage of education and would minimise the danger of repetition. Endless topic work on dinosaurs could be avoided. Children whose family moved house during their school life would be assured of not missing out on key elements of their education. Thirdly, with a national curriculum and accompanying tests, a school could be held accountable for what was taught and how well its pupils could learn. It would be possible to compare schools with each other, pinpoint the ones that were doing badly and devise a course of action to remedy the deficiency. In this way a country could be assured it was getting value for the public money invested in education. Ultimately a nation's core curriculum will reflect a particular balance of the aims listed above. The 1988 Education Act decreed a national curriculum for England, Wales and Northern Ireland. This can be used as a case study to test the case for a core curriculum.

THE NATIONAL CURRICULUM OF ENGLAND AND WALES

In 1988 a new National Curriculum for England, Wales and Northern Ireland, called an 'entitlement curriculum', was introduced. There were slight differences for Wales and Northern Ireland and these were developed further in Wales after Welsh devolution. It was a traditionalist curriculum of ten foundation subjects placed in a hierarchical list with the core subjects of English, Maths and Science at the top. The emphasis on science was particularly pertinent since, at the time, it was often a neglected subject and making it compulsory up to the age of sixteen opened up the subject to girls. These subjects were closely followed in importance by the 'other foundation' subjects, history, geography, technology, music, art and PE. At a later stage a modern foreign language was to be introduced. In addition all pupils were to be provided with religious education and a daily act of corporate worship. The curriculum was to be taught at different levels and with different degrees of emphasis depending on the age and ability of the child.

The government created ten subject consultation committees to aid with the creation of subject knowledge. Kenneth Baker, the then Secretary of State for Education, recalled in a newspaper interview that the time schedule was tight and that there were heated debates, particularly about what should be in English, History and Music. Whatever happened during these consultations, the final control of the curriculum content rested with the Secretary of State. The Rubicon had been crossed: in future no matter which government came to power it would have the authority to change the curriculum as it saw fit. The government was in fact decreeing what should count as knowledge.

NATIONAL TESTS

The real enforcer in relation to the National Curriculum was the introduction of national tests at seven, eleven and fourteen. Each subject had a programme of study with specific attainment targets. For each attainment target listed there were nine possible levels of attainment. The first seven indicate levels that any child might reach but level 8 indicates the achievement of very able pupils and level 9 'exceptional performance'. These helped the government keep tight control over the curriculum.

HOW SUCCESSFUL HAS THE NATIONAL CURRICULUM BEEN?

Positive evaluations of the National Curriculum have mainly been related to process. There is a feeling that the curriculum subjects are now more balanced with pupils unable to drop subjects early in their careers. There is evidence that schools themselves do more detailed planning and the curriculum has become clearer to all participants: pupils, teachers and parents. There is less danger of overlap and repetition. Pupils know what the syllabus is and how they are being taught. Teachers have a raised awareness of the importance of teaching methods and assessment. Parents know far more about their pupils' progress. These are not inconsiderable gains but the criticisms of the National Curriculum have been many, and of a fundamental nature. The curriculum was not neutral but contained important ideological and political messages. These became the basis of much of the criticism.

CRITICISM OF THE NATIONAL CURRICULUM

Subjects may have more equal time allotted as a result of the National Curriculum, but there have been criticisms of the subjects selected. This was a traditional curriculum based on what was originally perceived as a classical education. It took no account of new developments in knowledge and, on the whole, promoted little subject integration. Important subjects such as politics and the social sciences were completely excluded. In a democratic country it seemed extraordinary that pupils were getting little if any understanding of their own political system. Other countries in Europe made this a priority.

It was not just the subjects which caused concern. The content was seen as an even bigger problem as earlier accounts of the history curriculum have suggested. The teaching of English literature is another example. In 1988 the Conservatives wanted a return to classical texts and less emphasis on contemporary literature. Under Labour this was modified, but the Conservatives have returned to this theme in 2010. Critics have noted that the overall content of the National Curriculum focuses on England to the exclusion of other countries and has a particular world view which may be considered partisan and misleading.

The division of knowledge into attainment targets has also caused concern. Targets have been described as too specific and prone to see learning as progressing through a series of stages, one following the other, when in fact learning is more complex. The tests which have accompanied these targets have been highly criticised for their detrimental effect on children. Rather than giving more equality of opportunity, it is claimed, they have labelled children from an early age, ranking, differentiating and controlling them in a damaging way. Children who have not reached the recommended level for their age group are seen by themselves and others as failures. These issues are explored further in Chapter 5.

The curriculum has been modified in the twenty or so years since it was devised, but many of the criticisms still hold. It is seen as too specific, standardised and bureaucratic. There are few opportunities for regional and local interests to be portrayed. Students in higher education the author met were amazed and worried to find that, although coming from different parts of the country, they had all learnt precisely the same bits of information and consulted the same authorities in their learning. Overall the curriculum as it stands has been seen as stifling any possibility of innovation and this, it could be argued, is regressive. A world in constant flux and facing enormous difficulties needs students who have an eye to the future and who, through imagination, creative thinking and know-how, can help find some solutions. There appears to be little faith that the National Curriculum as it stands facilitates these skills.

WHO SHOULD CONTROL THE CURRICULUM?

THE POSITION IN ENGLAND TO DATE

It matters who controls the curriculum and who decides its content. A report by HM Inspectors in 1980 put the curriculum at the 'heart of education'. It noted that the world was changing. New skills were needed in response to global developments, but it also stated that 'neither the government nor the local authority should specify in detail what the schools should teach'. For the moment this was left to the 'professionalism of the teachers'. This did not last long and in England in 1988 control of the curriculum moved from teachers and local authorities to the government of the day who overturned the 1981 recommendations in favour of central state control. It was the first step in what has been described as the deprofessionalisation of teachers.

It has already been noted that politicians bring their own ideological slant to the task of deciding the curriculum. There is little evidence to suggest they take much notice of educational opinion. The independent primary review conducted by Jim Rose at the request of the Labour government, for example, made substantial recommendations for change in the primary curriculum, but these were subsequently dropped from the Children, Schools and Families Bill. The result has been a curriculum which is a highly centralised body of knowledge decided by politicians with little reference to the views of educators.

COULD EDUCATION BECOME PROPAGANDA?

School knowledge sanctioned by authority carries an assurance that it is in some way valid. Yet the curriculum always contains some attempt to persuade, whether it is through the selection of subject, content or pedagogical approach. Acceptance that the current curriculum is beyond criticism would be disturbing. What is to stop the curriculum ultimately becoming an exercise in propaganda, a situation where only certain facts are presented and where the audience is persuaded that this is the sole credible point of view?

One reason why Britain never had a national curriculum until 1988 was that earlier politicians feared the way totalitarian regimes – Nazi Germany and Soviet Russia – had used the curriculum as a means of extremist indoctrination. There are numerous examples of this happening. It has been used in the past to devastating effect. In the early 1900s a book appeared in Europe entitled *The Protocols of the Elders of Zion*. It was not an original work but rather a text cobbled together from earlier anti-Jewish writing,

Catholic tracts and other sources. It maintained that there was a Jewish conspiracy to take over the world. A good many supposedly sane people including academics and educationalists believed this propaganda. Hitler made it required reading in all German schools. It gave public support to horrendous state action.

Propaganda often goes hand in hand with indoxctrination. Indoctrination in schools occurs when pupils are not allowed to question what they are taught. It becomes part of the school socialisation/ social control programme. It happened in Nazi Germany. It happens today in China, Iran, North Korea and other totalitarian states, but it also occurs to some degree in all states where governments have control of the curriculum and where schools promote passive acceptance of what is taught, rather than encouraging strong critical responses. It would be wrong to describe the English National Curriculum as propaganda but unwise also to overlook its current slant or the potential for abuse. A centralised system, decided by politicians, controlled through examinations and accreditation with little room for manoeuvre or criticism, may not bode well for the future. The government said in 1988 that education was far too important to be left in the hands of teachers. Perhaps it is far too dangerous to be left in the hands of the politicians.

OTHER OPTIONS

But is this the only option? Would it be possible to have a core curriculum to which many more people contributed? In Norway a broad range of people form the curriculum consultancy committee. Parents, teachers, business and church leaders, politicians all have a say in what is taught. The result is an interesting document. It differs widely from the English version in that it is a slimmed down volume which outlines the various dimensions of the curriculum, including the spiritual, the creative and the social. It allows local contributions and does not specify levels or attainment targets. In France there is a much more centrally controlled curriculum but a large number of groups from across society have been involved in its creation. Safety lies in having individuals and groups with different angles and interests involved in the creation of the curriculum. Safety is enhanced if a curriculum is not all-encompassing and gives individual teachers the power to create their own responses.

SHOULD PARENTS HAVE A SAY?

An important aspect of this discussion is the power that parents should have in relation to the knowledge taught in school. After all, they consign their children to the school for a large part of their childhood. In any true democracy, should they not have a much bigger say in what is taught in schools? In the United States there is no national curriculum and parents in some states do have more influence. Parents who take a particular interest, however, often have strong ideological beliefs. This has important ramifications for a child's education since a powerful parent lobby can have a major impact on what is taught. Groups of fundamentalist Christians who did not believe in evolutionary theory gained control of the curriculum in Kansas. They had any mention of evolution removed from the state's science curriculum and from the graduation tests. This ruling was later reversed, but similar parents in other states are seeking to have creationism given equal status with evolutionary theory. As was indicated in Chapter 2, children sometimes need their family's views questioned and this is one of the tasks of education.

THE CURRICULUM PUPILS WOULD LIKE

To return to Burke and Grosvenor, pupils want a curriculum which is exciting, challenging and evolving. They want to be involved with their learning and see themselves as researchers finding things out for themselves. In *The School that I'd Like* in 1967 pupils disliked subject boundaries which they saw as too limiting, and this sentiment is replicated in the 2002 study in which students, recognise the need for some specialism but wanted a more holistic approach to learning.

The pupils' responses in 1967 chimed with the mood of the times. This was the year the Plowden Report on primary education was published. The report suggested that education should become more child-centred with pupils playing a more active part in deciding the curriculum. The pupils of 1967 were optimistic and hopeful that change would be coming to schools. Not so the children of 2002 who experienced a rigidity in the curriculum undreamt of in 1967. Their criticisms are incisive. A change has occurred since 1967 and pupils see themselves as global citizens.

They want a broader curriculum, one which introduces them to the wider world and encourages them to challenge the world they find themselves in, and to change it.

BEING CRITICAL OF WHAT WE ARE BEING TAUGHT

In order to recognize bias, pupils need from an early age to be encouraged to think critically. Critical thinking is a skill which can be taught, but it involves strategies which may be at odds with the traditional role of the school and the demands of the examination system. Critical thinking involves testing knowledge and ideas against a range of standards, making judgements on this basis and then taking action. There are a number of related skills. First is the process of asking good questions. 'Very young children do this naturally: 'What's it for?' 'How does it work?' 'Why are you doing that?' and so on. But the education system by and large does not favour this approach, and as children get older many lose the capacity to ask questions. The art of formulating an argument is an essential part of critical thinking, a skill which can be taught, and appears to be neglected in many schools. A few, but not many, students arrive in university with the ability to evaluate information and formulate a good argument.

The process of critical thinking allows pupils to identify flaws and prejudice; it permits them to examine their existing assumptions and enables them to make reasonable judgements about the facts and information they encounter; it is a protection against authoritarianism and indoctrination. At its best it allows practical consequences to ensue since all good thinking inevitably leads to attempts at problem solving: it is a basis for action. This of course has implications for pedagogy: the curriculum is intimately tied up with teaching and learning and it is with this premise that Chapter 5 will begin.

THE HIDDEN CURRICULUM

Apart from the official curriculum sociologists have identified that schools like other organisations have rules and expectations both implicit and explicit that impact upon pupils. Many of these are laid down by the school management and relate to such things as what pupils should wear and how they should behave. It is one of the teacher's jobs to relay these rules to the pupils. Sociologists have termed this the hidden curriculum. It is what pupils learn in school in addition to their recognized curriculum and one way through which the socialisation process takes place.

EFFECTS OF THE HIDDEN CURRICULUM

All schools have rules but there has been some debate as to the degree to which the rules are similar in all institutions. Is the hidden curriculum all-pervasive? Does it go further than socialisation to become in reality social control? Is it having an effect on pupils and through them on society at large? These questions are not easy to answer. We know from pupil accounts that there are many differences between schools, but there also appear to be striking similarities. Pupils have spoken strongly of the institutionalising effects of school, the repressive use of authority and the resulting inability of students to function without being told what to do. Some sociologists have confirmed this, arguing that there seems little negotiation between pupils and teachers and that the hidden curriculum is powerful and its effects are widely felt. Many individual teachers, they stress, would like to behave differently, but the institutionalising demands of the school do not permit it. School teaches that passive acceptance of events is better than active criticism, and that the voice of authority is often more important than independent personal judgement. It follows that pupils may learn that their own ideas are largely inconsequential.

THE HIDDEN CURRICULUM: LESS PERVASIVE THAN IMAGINED?

There is another school of thought which, while not minimising the power of the institution, argues that not all classrooms are the same. Despite the fact that similar rules pertain, individual teachers interpret them in different ways and this makes classrooms different from one another. Teachers and pupils at classroom level are engaged in working out a *modus operandi* for living together and what happens in individual classrooms is usually the result of negotiation between teacher and pupils. Teachers may set out their expectations of how the class will operate. Pupils test these expectations to see where the boundaries of acceptable behaviour are. This makes teachers rethink their expectations. New parameters for behaviour are established. In some classrooms the boundaries may be wide, in others narrower. In this way teachers and pupils together construct their own reality on a day-to-day basis. So the hidden curriculum may not be as repressive as some have maintained.

A CURRICULUM FOR UNIVERSITIES

Higher education institutions have traditionally been responsible for their own curricula. In the twentieth century universities and polytechnics, two sides of the so-called 'binary divide', offered different curricula, the universities academic degrees and the polytechnics vocational studies. After 1992 the binary divide disappeared: the polytechnics became universities and the academic/vocational split was ended. In any individual subject, the content may vary from university to university. However, there are safeguards on quality. The Quality Assurance Agency (QAA) periodically reviews the standards of programmes taught in higher education. All subjects have benchmarks. These are not precise curriculum specifications, but rather guidelines as to what a graduate should have achieved by the end of her/his course. They set out the principles by which the course must run, an overview of the kind of knowledge the course should be tackling and the skills it should be helping undergraduates to gain. This is not a national curriculum, however, since actual subject content is not prescribed and under current legislation the Secretary of State for Education is not allowed to determine the university curriculum

CONCLUSION

What we teach children in school, college and university is of vital importance to us all. It helps shape who we are as individuals and what kind of society we live in. What is taught in schools is not necessarily true, good or essential knowledge. It is a selection of knowledge chosen by interested parties at least in part to further their own ideological ends. In totalitarian states this can have devastating results. In a democratic society much depends on who has the power to set the curriculum and the degree of specificity which attends this. In England at the moment there is a National Curriculum which is politically driven, very specific and tested at every stage. It has largely sidelined teachers and pupils who have little say on content. The question is whether this a curriculum for the future? Will it produce students who are knowledgeable, creative and able to tackle the enormous problems which hover on the horizon? If not what should be done about it?

TEACHING, LEARNING
AND ASSESSMENT

MEET THE TEACHERS

IMAGES OF TEACHERS

So far our questions have revolved around the nature of schooling and what is being taught to whom. At the heart of this are the key people, the teachers. They are crucial because, in the end, they are the ones who interpret the curriculum and interact with the pupils. The lynchpin in the educational system, these are people whom students remember for a long time. They can have a powerful effect on their pupils, either for good or bad. In recent years there has been a growing recognition of their importance and the annual teaching awards for excellence have attempted to celebrate some of their achievements. So who are they and what do they think of their jobs? Are they the bogymen that some people remember, like the teacher from the television series *Grange Hill*, for example, who always had a sour expression, or perhaps the truly inspirational who have changed people's lives? Literature has provided us with numerous examples of teachers of different types. Memorable amongst these was Muriel Spark's Miss Jean Brodie, who was passionate about her beliefs and demonstrated the power that teachers can have in relation to pupils.

What images do we have of teachers? Thinking back to earlier school days can provoke strong memories, some good and others not so positive. Willard Walter Waller writing in 1932 in *The Sociology of Teaching* depicted the teaching profession as 'unsellable men and unmarriageable women'. These descriptions were in keeping with the spirit of the time, but the idea that teaching is a profession for those who cannot manage to do anything else lingers on in the old adage 'Those who can do, and those who can't teach'. This related in part to the time before teachers were required to have degrees, and women in particular applied to do teacher training because they were unlikely to secure a university place to do something considered more prestigious. Finally, there is the belief, perhaps fading of late, that teaching is a doddle, with short hours and long holidays.

WHO ARE THE TEACHERS?

Within the UK state system there are at present around 640,000 teachers,[1] 95 per cent of whom are of white ethnic background. They are almost equally divided, with some regional variations, between primary and secondary schools. There have always been more women than men being employed in teaching, but this trend is increasing. The vast majority of primary school teachers in the UK are female. Formerly heads of primary and secondary schools have tended to be men, but there is now a move towards more female heads. Most teachers have a degree in a chosen subject or subjects and a year's postgraduate teacher training (3 + 1), the latter being tightly government-controlled and inspected. To be a secondary teacher, a degree in the subject to be taught is required. Some universities are still running three or four year courses in which the teacher education is incorporated, mainly for primary teachers, but they are being phased out as the 3 + 1 option proves to be more cost effective.

WHY DO PEOPLE WANT TO BECOME TEACHERS?

Reasons are many and various. Individuals have different hopes of what jobs will offer and different expectations of what they will entail. Many teachers, particularly those in primary education, see their work as a vocation. They have been drawn to teaching because they want to work with children and believe they can have an impact on children's lives, improving their life chances; they are often dedicated and prepared to work long hours. This is the traditional view of the teacher, but in recent years other trends are emerging. Teaching is viewed as a career with opportunities for advancement. Working with children is important, but understanding the organisational structure of the school and advancing professionally is seen as a central component. A more instrumental approach can also be taken to the job. For some people, particularly women, teaching is a job which fits in well with having children. There are the same holidays and their own childcare needs are sometimes included. These categories are crude and by no means all-embracing or mutually exclusive, but they illustrate that all teachers do not come into teaching with the same outlook and that expectations of the job are likely to have an effect on performance.

IS TEACHING A PROFESSION?

The question is hotly debated, with many claims that government in taking away teachers' control of their working practices has deprofessionalised them. Before considering this, it is necessary to reflect on what a profession is. Originally it was a means of differentiating middle class from manual working class jobs. Gradually, however, the term has evolved: a professional is likely to have a high degree of skills and knowledge, often gained through a university degree. Professionals are expected to be without self-interest and to work conscientiously without supervision. They are expected to exhibit a degree of detachment from their jobs: they don't get emotionally involved. Under this description teaching might qualify as a profession. Teachers have qualifications, they tend to be altruistic and diligent, but beyond this there are problems with calling teaching a profession.

Firstly, because teaching involves close personal interaction with others, many teachers are emotionally involved with their jobs. Many invest a lot of themselves into their work and this can put them at risk. They are more vulnerable to threats to their self esteem and position than perhaps are people in other professions. Nowhere is this more obvious than in times of inspection. The

Office for Standards in Education (Ofsted), the body created to scrutinise education in England, inspects schools at periodic intervals. Unlike inspections in the past these events tend to be at short notice and fairly brutal in approach. As well as being a time of acute stress for teachers, causing confusion and anxiety, they create a sense that teachers have little input to educational policy and teaching methods. This has a deprofessionalising effect: teachers are no longer autonomous professionals.

Perhaps the most important defining feature of professionalism is the freedom to make decisions, the absence of external control and it on this point that critics have argued that the teaching profession is changing. All professionals are, in principle, accountable, either to peers, clients, government or any mixture of these, and professionals recognize the need for this. There is, however, considerable difference between accountability and control. Accountability involves giving a report of what has been done after the event, whilst control is to be supervised while in the act of doing something. Critics have maintained that since 1988 teaching has become a controlled job with little scope for individual initiative. In this way, are teachers becoming deskilled, with the considerable expertise that they used to have being lost?

Teachers, in the course of their careers, perform a variety of roles. They may be classroom or subject teachers to begin with, but later they may rise to be heads of department and eventually to being deputy or head teachers. In schools in the UK all teachers also have a strong pastoral role and there are opportunities for advancement in taking on whole-school roles.

SUPPORT WORKERS

There have always been support workers in school but in the past they have mainly done administrative jobs. Since 2002 however there has been a huge growth in the number of teaching assistants (TAs). These personnel are not qualified teachers but they support teachers by working with small groups of children, helping pupils with special needs, preparing materials for teaching and doing other similar tasks. Higher level teaching assistants (HLTA) now do some class teaching and are more involved with pupils' learning. There are a number of courses they can do to get qualified. The original idea, conceived by the then education minister Estelle Morris, was to reduce teachers' workloads by providing further classroom support. Thus teachers should have more time for lesson preparation. A controversy has always surrounded this policy. It was seen by some teachers' unions as a way of further deprofessionalising the teaching force and devaluing the work of teachers. An extensive investigation into the role of teaching assistants conducted by Peter Blatchford and others in 2009, *Deployment and Impact of Support Staff in Schools*, found that support staff were potentially playing a positive role in school. Their work with individual children had reduced disruptive behaviour in secondary schools. Overall however there was little difference in learning gains between those pupils who were helped and those who were not. In this as in other surveys, questions were raised about how the assistants were deployed and the lack of training given to teachers in relation to this.

TEACHING AND LEARNING

TEACHING

Teachers teach and children learn. It seems quite straightforward, but how sure can we be of the connection between teaching and learning? The idea of every child being taught in institutions for most of the working day up to and beyond the age of eighteen is a new idea. Why is it needed and have pupils benefited from it? Do children not learn by themselves anyway? Do they really need active tuition? This question has dogged teaching ever since the introduction of compulsory schooling. The key question must be how do people learn best and to what degree does school aid or frustrate this process? Teaching and learning are intimately bound together: what it means to be a teacher depends one's view of children as learners.

PEDAGOGY

'Pedagogy' can be described simply as the process of teaching. It has its roots in Greek where it meant 'to lead the child' and in Latin where it referred to 'child instruction'. In modern times it has come to cover a wide range of teaching activities including the design of lessons, strategies to encourage effective learning and different methods of teaching. It has been portrayed as both an art and a science, the latter suggesting that it is a systematic enterprise accompanied by the development of relevant theory and practice. Pedagogy would seem to be of key importance in any education system, but in the UK overall it has received surprisingly little attention. Unlike the European tradition which has been strong in this respect, England retained a scepticism about the value of a science of teaching. Despite changes, particularly in the last twenty years it is difficult to identify any overall pedagogical approaches. Historically, the art of teaching did not figure strongly in postgraduate teacher training courses. There was a belief that teaching is best left to the individual who will, with her charisma and intuition, develop her own way of doing the job. There was also a belief that teachers were born to the job. They either had the necessary abilities to be a good teacher or they didn't, and there was little training could do to affect this. That teachers are by and large not taught to teach seems surprising but there are reasons for it, some of which are social and political and others which are related to the psychology of learning.

PEDAGOGY AND FORMAL SCHOOLING

In 1870, with the introduction of elementary education for all, there was a flurry of interest in how to teach, but it was mostly confined to work done by some local authorities in large cities. It was based on a belief that children would stay in the same school throughout their schooling and there would be no division between elementary and secondary schools. With the development of separate schools at eleven, interest in pedagogy declined and, consequently, no national system developed. For a long time it was believed that real learning did not take place in primary schools. Children were just being socialised and early-years education was largely childminding. It has taken a long time for the UK to recognise the crucial importance of the first years of education and the enormous effect they can have on future performance. In secondary schools pedagogy was a neglected study because it was originally modelled on public schools' practice. Public school masters did not require teaching certificates to teach. The sole qualification necessary was an academic degree. State-sponsored secondary education followed this route, with pedagogy considered equally unimportant. Teachers would work out their own method of teaching, and any suggestion that teaching itself could be taught was often decried.

EARLIEST FORMS OF TEACHING

In the earliest state schools teaching was largely 'didactic': teachers relayed to pupils the content of the lesson. Teachers were seen as the font of all knowledge, occasionally supported by sanctioned textbooks, and their job was to impart this knowledge to the pupils in their charge. Associated with this was the belief that children are born with empty minds which it was the teacher's job to fill; the role of the pupil was largely passive. Although this pervaded all levels of education, it took different forms in different kinds of schools.

Pictures of the earliest state schools often show row after row of young children sitting facing the teacher and listening intently – or not – to what they are being told. Sometimes quite small children are fast asleep. Rote learning and practice of what was learnt were key elements of the classroom experience. There was little chance of creative expression and education was largely confined to the classroom. The design of school buildings of the time reflected these methods with classrooms with windows high up in the walls so that the outside world would not intrude on classroom life and distract the children. The accent was very much on class competition, with the higher achievers being pitched against the younger ones, the class often sitting in rows according to their overall class position. Teachers needed knowledge, an understanding of discipline and little else to perform this role.

In some public schools, however, a different version of teaching pervaded. This was related to theories of the mind which were current at the time. One strand of this has argued that in order for learning to take place, the mind needs to be exercised, disciplined and trained. This training of the mind it was believed would be an excellent preparation for dealing with the vicissitudes of life and could best be done through the study of such subjects as Latin,

Greek and geometry. This contributed to the development of the idea of a classical education which originated in the Greco-Roman world and was reinterpreted in the *Gymnasia* of Germany and the grammar schools of England and Wales. An important part of this view of learning was the Socratic method where the teacher, rather than imparting knowledge, seeks to draw out what is in the learner's mind through question and answer.

PEDAGOGY AND INTELLIGENCE

Ideas about the nature of intelligence outlined in Chapter 1 also affected teaching. The theory of intelligence which initially prevailed related to a belief that there were definite limits to achievement. A child is born with a certain genetic inheritance and the environment does little to affect this. The intelligent will learn anyway and the less intelligent have only limited potential. If this were true, little could be altered by anything a teacher could do and teaching would be largely irrelevant. These ideas were central to educational thinking and prevailed in the UK up until the 1970s. In some areas their legacy remains. It is interesting to note that in other countries a different pedagogy arose, partly because schooling remained largely unaffected by the intelligence debate. In Japan for example, there is a belief that all children are infinitely malleable. Teachers do not have a picture in their heads of the average child having an IQ of 100 and others being above or below this; all children are thought of as being capable of success. Of course, there are other factors too, such as belief in the importance of hard work, which contribute to high rates of success in Japanese education; but the idea that all children can succeed is pervasive.

PEDAGOGY AND PROGRESSIVE THINKING

Another challenge to pedagogy came from progressive education which is examined in detail in Chapter 6. In brief the proponents of progressive education had the firm belief that pupils develop and learn autonomously. Adults only aid or frustrate the process, but don't actually play a leading role in learning. The aim of the educator at best was to 'follow the child' and, although there were numerous examples of how to do this, pedagogy as an art did not warrant further consideration. It was only when the psychology of learning began to change dramatically that pedagogy became more important. So what exactly is learning and how does it relate to what happens in school?

LEARNING

Learning is the process by which humans and animals acquire new knowledge, skills and understanding. But what do we know of this process that is so commonplace that we almost overlook it? From a very early age infants display curiosity and the desire to learn. Indeed there is evidence to suggest that learning begins before birth with babies able to recognize the tunes their mothers listened to while pregnant. In the past children have mostly learnt from adults, parents and teachers and from their peers, but the world has changed. Pupils frequently have easy access to knowledge that their parents would find hard to locate. Even small children initiated into the digital age have become rapidly more expert than their parents. Most very young children appear to learn almost effortlessly, but by the time they are in school the process seems fraught with difficulties. It raises questions about what are the optimum conditions for learning. How can teachers interact with children to promote learning?

LEARNING BY TRIAL AND ERROR

Early theories of learning which dominated the first half of the twentieth century were often based on behaviourist psychology. People, it was believed, learn by trial and error and learning is reinforced by getting satisfactory results These conclusions were based on the work done by Ivan Pavlov, a Russian scientist living at the beginning of the twentieth century. In his famous experiments with dogs, Pavlov established that the animals could be conditioned to change their behaviour. Although at first they only salivated at the sight and smell of food, if the food was brought by lab technicians, people in white coats, then the appearance of the people in coats without the food was sufficient to provide salivation. A US psychologist, Burrhus Skinner, extended these experiments, conditioning rats to press levers in order to get food. Dogs and rats may seem far from the classroom but these theories about learning have been employed in school. Skinner felt that many of these strategies could be used with children. He suggested that much of the schooling he witnessed depended on punishment and ridicule. Lessons and examinations were largely targeted at revealing what pupils didn't know rather than what they did know. These were not, he thought, optimum conditions for producing learning. Teachers were failing to shape their pupils' behaviour successfully. Learning comes from the reinforcement of connections between stimulus and response.

Behaviour modification was a technique developed in schools to deal with undesirable pupil behaviour. The theory holds that individuals react better to praise than to punishment; so this system offers praise every time a desirable action is observed. It has been used mostly in relation to behaviour rather than to cognitive learning. In a weak form it can be seen in the smiley faces or stars which are appended to children's work which the teacher thinks has been well done.

Although these theories presented tools for teachers and helped to focus on the pedagogy of the classroom, they raised serious worries. Were external reward and reinforcement necessary to promote learning? Given the right conditions could pupils learn for themselves? Thoughts of this kind led to the major steps forward in learning theory which have informed primary education in the UK during the last thirty years.

CHILDREN AS ACTIVE LEARNERS: THE CONSTRUCTIVIST REVOLUTION

While not disparaging some of the good work that behaviour modification has achieved, it became increasingly depressing to view children as being in the same category as rats. The psychology of learning was about to change dramatically with the advent of Jean Piaget, Lev Vygotsky and Jerome Bruner. Intelligence is not fixed they said: it is a product of genetic inheritance and the impact of the environment. It follows that no child's potential is set in stone. Bruner famously said that any subject can be taught to anyone one at any age in some form that is both interesting and honest. Education, properly done, can help people reach their full potential.

Children are active in their learning, constantly making sense of the world in which they find themselves. They do not come to the classroom with empty minds. They come to each new experience with a wealth of experience from their past. They bring to school ways of understanding the world they have learnt from home. This knowledge may be hazy, incomplete or on occasion even wrong, but it is the point which teachers need to connect to. These understandings link with those raised in Chapter 2 on the importance of respecting and understanding a child's family of origin and culture.

Children make sense of what is currently happening by making links with what they already know. In this way they are agents in the active construction of knowledge. The key to understanding comes from making good connections. How these connections are made is, however, a matter of some dispute. Piaget, a French biologist, saw children almost as lone scientists exploring their world. From the observation of young boys Piaget postulated that children learnt best through self-directed problem solving. Realising the consequences of their actions was the key to learning. He emphasised the importance of action and problem solving. Abstract thinking, he said, is rooted in practical experiences. Moreover, learning does not rest on external motivating factors – the promise of rewards – but rather for young children, mastering the problem is what matters.

LEARNING IN STAGES AND THE CONCEPT OF READINESS

Piaget observed that sometimes people learn things easily and at other times have more difficulty. He attributed this to their stage of development. For Piaget, children think in a different way from adults. They start off at birth learning intuitively, but then pass through a number of stages, each one involving major changes in the way they think. Children's ability to understand and progress depends on their having reached the right stage of intellectual ability. Only when they have passed through a series of stages do they reach a point where they can reason and understand in a rational way. Learning depends on the mastering of preceding steps.

This led to the concept of 'readiness': children can only be taught if they have reached the right stage in their development. To a certain extent these ideas were supported by progressive educators who claimed that children should set their own pace of learning, only doing what they themselves considered appropriate. Teachers, however, frequently associated readiness with having appropriate speech and social manners, and readiness became more a matter of being in the right social class than having reached the right stage of development. What followed from this was that those 'ready to learn' were taught more than those deemed not yet 'ready'. These labels had an effect both on the pupils themselves and the ways teachers perceived them. Those identified as not yet ready to learn rarely caught up with their peers.

Stages of development is an interesting psychological construct which has had a strong influence on modern schooling. Learning has tended to be viewed as sequential. This idea is now built into the National Curriculum with most children being expected to reach certain stages at key points in their schooling. In some countries progression from one class to the next is dependent on reaching a certain level in every subject. In the United States for example pupils are held down a year if they do not meet the specific achievements. Even though this does not happen in England there is still a feeling that children who have failed to reach the prescribed level need to rectify their failings fairly quickly. But does learning really proceed in this orderly fashion? Sometimes there seems good reason for children to grasp the meaning of one concept before moving on to another but at other times it is obvious that learning does not progress tidily.

LEARNING IS A SOCIAL ACTIVITY

Whilst accepting and celebrating many of Piaget's findings, Bruner and Vygotsky disagreed with him in a number of important ways. Bruner saw humans as being deeply embedded in their particular cultures. Education reflects this, not just in the curriculum content, but by influencing the very way we make sense of our world. Language is an important factor: our mother tongue structures the way we think. Education, therefore, has to be viewed as a social activity. Children do not learn in isolation from others; their relationship to their peers and to adults is crucial. Language and communication are of key importance. For Vygotsky the child learns by interacting with more knowledgeable adults. He called this the zone of proximal development which is the difference between what a child can learn on her own and what she learns with the help of more knowledgeable adults. Bruner suggested that interaction between peers is also important. Children learn from interaction with other children. These findings are borne out by classroom events. The experience of explaining a concept to somebody else often helps children clarify their own thinking. Beyond this, Bruner maintained that children working together can construct answers which they can't arrive at by working alone. These ideas have important implications for pedagogy. Whereas Piaget had seen teaching as a marginal enterprise in the development of learning capacity, for Bruner and Vygotsky it was of central importance.

STRUCTURE AND SCAFFOLDING

Perhaps one of the key contributions of constructivists to education is the stress on the importance of structure. Bruner maintained that children learn best when they understand the structure of a subject. Rather than learning facts and figures, pupils need to understand the essential ideas on which the subject is based. What is the heart of the matter? This needs to be returned to over and over again, but not always in the same form. This contributed to the concept of the 'spiral curriculum' in which the teacher revisits the basic ideas repeatedly but in different ways.

For Bruner it wasn't just learning the structure of a subject which was important. It was also getting actively involved in understanding how a professional in that subject would pursue further knowledge. The learner needs to understand the intention and motives behind the work. To do this he has to take on the role of the person concerned. In the case of history which was discussed in Chapter 4, the child has to understand what being a historian really means: what excites them and how they do their work. This potential for excitement needs to be programmed into the learning. It is the process of *being* a historian which is important for the learner rather than memorisation of historical facts.

For the constructivists it is not just the curriculum which needs structure, however, teachers themselves can aid children's learning initially by providing scaffolding, that is buttressing learning by providing support for pupils. This help can come in a number of ways, ranging from verbal encouragement to the asking of key questions and the modelling of reasonable answers. Teachers were back at centre stage, but in a rather different way from the first forms of teaching. They were not there to transmit knowledge any more, but to facilitate learning. Redefining the nature of learning had effects on classroom practice.

CHANGES IN CLASSROOM PRACTICE

PLOWDEN

The 1960s saw the beginning of radical changes in primary education. The influences of Piaget and the progressive education movement were beginning to filter through to schools. These trends were brought together with the publication of the Plowden Report in 1967. The report included the statement 'At the heart of the educational process lies the child.' It attempted to make primary education child-centred and focused more on how pupils learn than on what they are taught. It broke with traditional education by challenging the role of the teacher and suggesting that there should be far more flexibility in the way the curriculum was planned. Learning should be active and pupils should discover things for themselves by hands-on experience. Play was to be a crucial element in the curriculum. Plowden suggested that ideally learning should be more individualised and tailored to the needs of each child. There was less concern with the outcomes of learning and with assessment. These ideas changed the way primary schools were organised. Traditional classrooms were self contained units where the teacher reigned supreme. The new order called for more open plan areas, more access to the outside world and more opportunities for teachers to teach together. The classroom rows were abandoned and children were seated in groups so that they could interact with one another.

Not all these ideas were enthusiastically received, however. Much depended on the local authority. Oxfordshire and Leicestershire Local Authorities, for example, became key exponents of child-centred education and visitors came from around the world to view the new developments. Many teachers in other parts of the country, however, retained practices associated with traditional methods. Plowden had called for the curriculum to be individualised but in reality this was impossible to achieve, and indeed the report itself had conceded this, indicating that pupils might be taught in groups as a compromise. IQ and ability became strongly related to the groups pupils were in. Fresh ideas about pedagogy also failed to emerge.

POLITICAL BACKLASH

The scene was set for a battle: political heavyweights and the media weighed in to add their pronouncements to the general melee. Arguments were raised about the relative merits of each approach and as with most things relating to schooling they took on a political hue. Traditional methods, the right claimed, represented the best in pedagogy. Progressive methods were the result of the decadent 1960s and contained little merit. Children finding things out for themselves was a recipe for disaster, giving the less committed pupils a chance to waste their days. The debate was not helped by the notorious case of the William Tyndale Junior School in the London Borough of Islington which dominated the press for nearly six months in 1975/76. The school practised so-called progressive methods allowing children maximum choice as to how they should spend their days. As far as the critics were concerned the children were running wild. It raised the ominous question of who was really running schools. The *Black Papers*, a series of pamphlets written by Brian Cox and Tony Dyson, were an indictment of progressive methods and they confirmed the public view that schools were out of control. Lacking an explicit pedagogy which had been rationally arrived at and widely promulgated, education was not able to defend itself from such attacks.

RESEARCH ON TEACHING METHODS: WHICH IS BEST?

Which method of pedagogy works best for the children? In 1975 Neville Bennett, a researcher at the University of Lancaster, produced a book entitled *Teaching Styles and Pupil Progress*. He compared formal approaches to teaching with more progressive approaches and came to the conclusion overall that 'formal' primary methods were the more effective. These results were combined with various caveats such as, for example, the most successful teacher in his research used progressive methods. Very little consideration was given to the detail of the book which contained interesting and sometimes contradictory findings. The headline was enough as Bennett himself ruefully recalled returning to Heathrow just after the book's publication and being swamped by the media.

The overall results of this research sound comforting. Traditional methods with some minor modifications are best; but best for what? Bennett was assessing learning gains in reading, maths and English. He also calculated the amount of time pupils spent on-task. In most cases pupils did better when formally instructed. It would be wrong to disparage these findings but the research raises a number of questions. Are the aims of education solely to be measured in terms of basic skills in English and maths? What effect does formal teaching have on the development of lifelong interest in a topic?

A flurry of research findings in the 1970s including an HMI survey in 1978 and the ORACLE research of the 1980s led by Maurice Galton and Brian Simon found that on the whole teachers had not adopted progressive methods. Both surveys found that there was little evidence of group or exploratory work in primary classrooms, and the most common feature noted was whole class teaching and individual work. The research also found that most teachers had their classrooms well under control, but that many primary teachers spent too much time trying to teach individuals in an attempt to respond to Plowden's message about child-centred education.

PEDAGOGY RETHOUGHT

The debates over traditional versus progressive education did bring pedagogy back into the limelight and schools quietly began to change. The views of Bruner and Vygotsky began to influence what went on in the classroom. It made the process of talking and listening far more important, whether it was talking with the teacher, a peer or in groups. Cognitive mapping, which helps pupils to identify important concepts, has also aided learning. In some classrooms there has been a concentration on co-operative learning and the advantages that this brings. There was now an understanding that creating a rigid division between formal and informal teaching is harmful to children's learning. There are times when children need to discover things for themselves and other times when more formal teaching may be beneficial, but much depends on the quality of the pedagogy.

PACIFIC RIM COUNTRIES DO WELL

As far as pedagogy was concerned relative peace was to be short-lived. The early 1990s saw a moral panic in relation to standards of numeracy and literacy. Put simply, in international comparisons the Pacific Rim countries were doing better than England and the United States. This led to US reports suggesting that state education was on the way to cataclysmic disaster. American pupils, it was claimed, had low expectations and spent less time studying than did students in other industrialised countries. Similar concerns were expressed in England. What was actually happening in Pacific Rim countries to warrant their success? Attention focused on pedagogy. Investigations in South Korea suggested that what contributed to pupil progress was a combination of whole class teaching, checking that pupils had understood what had been taught and ensuring that the whole class was moving forward together. An HMI visit to Japanese schools in 1992 endorsed these results. Pupil made the best progress when lessons are divided into three parts. The teacher explains things clearly, the pupils do a task together and some work on their own and finally the teacher pulls the threads together. It was time to learn the lessons from abroad.

THE GOVERNMENT STEPS IN

Having already taken control of the curriculum, subsequent governments moved on to take control of pedagogy. In 1992 the Conservatives stated that there should be more class teaching, more specialist subject teaching and that there should be streaming and grouping by attainment. But in 1998 New Labour went further than this and introduced national strategies for literacy and numeracy with prescribed teaching methods. These consisted of the one-hour three-part lesson with interactive class teaching in English and literacy every day for every pupil. In recent years the government has intervened further in pedagogy by suggesting that there is only one way to teach reading, and this is through 'synthetic phonics': learning letter sounds systematically before reading a text. They have gone on to use punitive measures against university departments who fail to convey this to their PGCE trainees. While there is evidence of some success in teaching reading in this way, there are other ways of doing it and teachers are resisting the reliance on one method of teaching.

In England pedagogy has failed to develop a strong base and has been dogged by a lack of a means to do this. Individualism has prevailed throughout. The General Teaching Council for England was instituted, but its remit was limited and the 2010 coalition government abolished it. There is no body dedicated to the promotion of a pedagogy based on solid research. Schools are, therefore, left to the whim of the politicians of the day and the influence of the media.

OTHER FACTORS WHICH INFLUENCE TEACHING AND LEARNING

EXPECTATIONS

The psychology of learning has important insights for pedagogy, but there are other factors which affect teaching and learning in classrooms. Social psychology has indicated how expectations affect performance. Teachers and pupils come to the classroom with a number of preconceived ideas as to what is likely to happen and these expectations play a considerable part in the process of teaching and learning. Teachers usually have 'working predictions' of the way things will be in the classroom. In particular in the UK, they have definite beliefs about which groups of children are likely to succeed. These expectations are affected by a whole number of characteristics not directly related to academic ability. Research has demonstrated that pupil personality, physical attractiveness, speech characteristics, writing neatness, seating location, and even first names, may affect a teacher's perception of what constitutes a potentially successful student.

Pupils at school are in the process of developing a self-image. The younger the pupil the less clear they are of their identity. As they get older these images harden into what may be seen as a 'life script': a way of predicting what will happen to them and how they are likely to react to given situations. These scripts come in part from what they learn about themselves in a school setting. Teachers can confirm or challenge these scripts. Evidence suggests that most pupils want to do well, but that their performance can be affected by beliefs their teachers hold about them. An image of oneself as a poor learner or as non-academic can have a disastrous effect on achievement.

A famous study in 1970 by Ray Rist of an urban ghetto school traced the impact of expectations on subsequent classroom behaviour in the first year of schooling. He noted that the children were divided by teachers very rapidly — within eight days of their first entry into school — into groups of those children who were expected to learn and those who were not. These expectations were often based not on ability but on the children's speech, appearance and social background. The children caught the messages and produced the appropriate behaviour, thus confirming the teachers' original expectations. The groups became rigid sets by the end of the year with pupils and subsequent teachers believing that these groups were strongly related to individual ability. Research by Robert Rosenthal and Lenore Jacobson in 1968, *Pygmalion in the Classroom*, outlined the effect of self-fulfilling prophecies. They gave pupils a test and identified a group who would 'bloom' in the next six months. These pupils were not in reality the brightest group in the class but both they and their teachers believed what they had been told. At the end of the school year these pupils had performed the best. This research raised the question of the degree to which teacher expectations affect pupils' achievement. It led to further investigations into what images teachers have of good and poor pupils.

WHAT CONSTITUTES A GOOD PUPIL?

Teachers have strong images of what constitutes a good pupil and they often subconsciously measure the pupils they encounter against this model. In the main they prefer attentive, conforming, quiet, easy-to-handle pupils. It is not difficult to see why. With busy, sometimes stressful, lives teachers are likely to give more credibility to those who are relatively compliant. But is a good pupil the same as a good learner? Are the young people identified as good pupils really good learners? Perhaps this has nothing to do with learning and everything to do with making teachers' lives a bit easier.

Staff development work done in a South Wales secondary school and reported by Kay Wood and Pat Millichamp set out to explore these issues further. When teachers were asked to identify good pupils they chose the quiet hard-working ones, who turned out to be overwhelmingly middle class girls. Bad pupils were described as disruptive, pushing boundaries, trying to divert the teacher from the task in hand, distracting their peers, quick to argue and prone to confrontation. They were often perceived by the teachers as being on the edge of rebellion and were in the main working class boys. Close observation of the identified pupils demonstrated that good pupils were actually those who functioned well in the traditional school set-up. Poor pupils did not. The school intervened and did away with the normal curriculum for two weeks. Students had to set their own tasks for the fortnight and find their own solutions. Teachers acted as guides and facilitators only. The results were interesting. Pupils who had previously been designated poor did exceedingly well. In addition the absentee rate which had been high for this group fell dramatically. The pupils who found the exercise the hardest were the previously successful girls.

There still remained, however, a core of poor learners with low levels of skill whom the teachers had difficulty empathising with. In staff development sessions the teachers were asked to do tasks which, unknown to them, were deliberately set for failure. Overall the tasks created widespread panic and the staff began to reconnect again with what challenges learning poses for some pupils. Some teachers even apologised to their students. What was also interesting was that during the course of the exercise those teachers not succeeding rapidly became disruptive and noisy, not unlike their own descriptions of poor pupils.

PUPIL VIEWS ON TEACHING AND LEARNING

Pupils have clear views on teaching and learning which are remarkably consistent over time. Teachers have a strong effect on pupils' lives and Jean Rudduck and Donald McIntyre report that there is a considerable agreement by pupils as to what constitutes a good teacher. Pupils value, above all else, a teacher who is cheerful, has a good sense of humour and understands what it means to be a young person in today's world. They want teachers who show them respect, treat everyone fairly and offer praise when it is warranted. The capacity to listen to pupils is very important. These skills rank more highly than having good subject knowledge. On the surface they may appear to be personal characteristics, but in actual fact they are often indicators of professional expertise. The ability to establish good personal relationships is top of the pupils' list of what makes a good teacher.

Pupils' evaluations of learning experiences tally closely with the findings of constructivist psychologists. The role of the teacher is to provide clear and coherent explanations which are strongly connected to what pupils know already. Pupils want active participation. They want to find things out for themselves. They want to run research projects, collect evidence, do experiments. They want good class discussion. They express a need for far more autonomy in relation to learning than they are currently given. They value lessons which are well prepared with a clear focus and where the delivery is varied and well paced, particularly those where the teacher is clearly interested in what she is teaching.

Pupils constantly reiterate that their experience of school is of tedium and the rote learning of facts, the purpose of which is lost to many of them. Pupils themselves recognize that learning is becoming more limited and rapidly turning into a commodity the sole purpose of which is to obtain exam results. They want education to be meaningful, lively and relevant to living in the modern world. The learning they are engaged with needs to present a constant intellectual challenge. These views are worth listening to, and it is perhaps the tragedy of modern education that little account is paid to them.

The remarkable thing about the research done into pupils' views is not the degree of thoughtfulness and maturity that students bring to the discussion, but the degree to which their voices are constantly overlooked. From the 1960s to the present day their views have been solicited, but in very few ways acted upon. Yet pupils are the experts. It is they who spend day after day in the same classrooms, who constantly observe what is going on and who are on the receiving end of education. When asked, they are able to comment succinctly on the kind of teaching they are receiving and the learning opportunities which are on offer. They can be very positive in praising the delivery of good lessons, but are also keen to point out what could be improved and how this could be done. They recognise that there are different points of view and frequently attempt to see things from the teacher's perspective.

ASSESSMENT

As has been noted in Chapter 2, one of schooling's main functions is to provide pupils with certification when they finish education. The purpose of this is in principle to sort out those with the most potential and to channel them into appropriate jobs. To some extent this has always been the case. In recent years, though, the need for certification has been rising. We are requiring more and more documentation to do jobs which, perhaps, in earlier times did not require exam passes or certificates at all. The role of assessment in school is therefore of key importance. From nursery to university pupils are being constantly assessed. It is a major part of school life. The assessment comes in a variety of forms: the looks and gestures teachers give, the work they mark, classroom competitions and tests and exams. It can have far-reaching effects on pupils' lives. Good education encompasses good assessment because it is appropriate that both learners and teachers should be curious about what learning has taken place and whether the learning outcomes have been achieved. But what do we mean by good assessment? Assessment like all other aspects of education is not an objective science. Choosing between different methods of assessment involves debate about the nature and purpose of education.

SUMMATIVE ASSESSMENT

The most obvious assessments in school are the formal examinations which measure final achievement. These are known as *summative* assessments because they seek to grade, select and predict future performance. They come in the form of public and national examinations, the nature of which has changed over time. Unseen formal examination questions have now been supplemented by coursework, essays and projects. These changes seem to have favoured girls, with boys performing less well. They have also brought worries about their reliability and about the opportunities for teachers and parents unfairly to affect outcomes. In universities, once the epicentres of formal assessment, examinations have all but disappeared, with work being continuously assessed. There are constant debates about the value of examinations.

Examinations. A case has been made for examinations because, on the whole, they are less likely to incur cheating. They measure certain skills well such as the ability to answer concisely and rapidly. Above all they focus pupils' attention on the subject matter in hand and, in universities, are seen to encourage attendance. Some pupils undoubtedly prefer them as they suit their learning styles. Many university lecturers also like them because on the whole they tend to be briefer than other assessments and easier to mark. There are, however, an equal number of objections to examinations. It is claimed that they are frequently inaccurate in that they can be badly marked, and when the student's name is displayed the work of male candidates has been more favourably received. They only represent a small part of what a person can do and being held on a particular day they may not be a very valid measure even of that. They often measure recall only, rather than in-depth understanding of the subject. They offer an extrinsic reward for learning, rather than encouraging the desire to learn for its own sake. Much depends on the type of examination in question. Answers to questions written in essay form are not the only means of formal assessment. Multiple choice questions, practical tests, problem solving all appear in final assessments. In the end, summative assessment stands or falls on the degree to which it offers a fair representation of what a pupil has achieved.

FORMATIVE ASSESSMENT

There is another type of assessment which frequently happens in schools. *Formative* assessment measures progress, diagnoses problems and gives both students and teachers an indication as to how teaching and learning are progressing. This type of assessment comes in the form of the written work which is marked by the teacher, but also in the classroom interactions which occur daily. It comes in the questions teachers ask of the class and the formal feedback which pupils get. Pupils however frequently view assessment in very different ways from that of the teacher. Most pupils are overwhelmingly concerned with knowing what marks they have got and relating these to the marks of their peers. In that sense they see assessment as summaries of their achievement not indicators of how to improve their work. It is something that is 'done' to them by and for others. Students often see themselves as outsiders looking in on an obscure process which is part of the mystery of teaching. These attitudes are often based on ignorance of how teachers are marking their work. On the whole, assessment is for many pupils not a pleasant or particularly satisfying experience. Memories of schooling are strong in relation to this. The piece of work done on page 1 of the exercise book, dotted with red underlining and crosses, is there for ever more, the first thing to be seen on opening the book and a constant reminder of one's failure.

Children in England are among the most assessed in the world. Report after report highlights the negative effects this is having on pupils, including ever-increasing levels of stress and even, for some children, suicide. The Task Group on Assessment and Testing (TGAT) formed to set up the assessment of the National Curriculum argued that Standard Assessment Tasks (SATs) were to measure attainment to date and were not to be used as a predication for future performance. There is evidence to suggest, however, that this is not how they are viewed by pupils or teachers. Not doing well in these national tests is regarded both as a present failure and as a measurement of future potential. For many children assessment becomes a barrier rather than a help to learning. It makes getting the right response, whether in classroom question-and-answer sessions or in written tests, an absolute priority. It rules out taking risks. But this is not how any of us learn. Knowledge itself progresses through mistakes acknowledged and celebrated. Science makes advances through trying things out and recognizing errors. Assessment has to be more than a summative judgement if it is ever to impact on learners.

SCHOOL ACCOUNTABILITY

One of the main reasons for the high levels of assessment in English schools is the wish to make schools accountable for their own performance. They provide a way for schools to be monitored and teaching evaluated. At one level, however, these are crude measures of effectiveness. The absence of a single secondary school teacher for any period of time can depress exam results and lead to a fall in overall school performance. This can have knock-on effects on the school's funding. Wales has abolished this form of testing in recent years and it is largely absent in the Scottish education system. In Europe overall increased levels of funding have led to more demands for increased accountability, but this is rarely measured by pupil tests. The Scandinavian countries which have high levels of pupil achievement utilise few formal tests but invest considerably in good formative assessment.

CONCLUSION

This chapter has focused on teaching, learning and assessment. Teachers remain probably the most crucial element in schooling but their role is changing. There are concerns that they are becoming deprofessionalised, with consequences for both teachers and pupils. In England and Wales, unlike elsewhere in Europe, there has been an absence of a recognized and accepted pedagogy. There are a number of reasons for this. The first is the belief that good teaching is largely intuitive and cannot, itself, be taught. The second was the fact that the earliest forms of teaching were modelled on that of the public schools where knowledge rather than the ability to teach was the most important factor. Finally the dominance of certain beliefs about intelligence did not encourage or facilitate an active role for teachers.

In recent years there have been important developments in learning theory particularly those associated with the constructivist views of learning, but it is difficult to determine the precise impact these have had on schooling. With increased central control in the last twenty years, teaching and learning have come to be determined more and more by the dictate of governments.

Assessment is an important feature of education. It comes in a variety of forms, with formative assessment being the most useful in promoting learning. In England at the moment there is a stress on summative assessment with English pupils being amongst the most tested in the world. There is an on-going debate about the merit and benefits of national testing on this scale

ALTERNATIVE VIEWS OF EDUCATION

The previous chapters have largely concentrated on state schooling because, in developed and emerging countries, the majority of students encounter this 'standard' formal education. However, over the last 300 years or so, philosophers, educationalists and parents have challenged current thinking on education and schooling. They have had very different ideas about the nature of children and how they learn and, as a result, have often condemned official forms of schooling. Not only have they written about their views but have also tried them out. In the last century educators have established their own schools outside the state system, and many still survive and flourish. Other groups have felt that state education on its own is insufficient and have set up additional schooling to help their children. There are those who go further, regarding state schooling as so harmful that they choose to educate their children at home. In recent times, however, there has been a change of emphasis. Challenge is not just coming from outside the system; there is now an unprecedented chorus of criticism of modern-day schooling and this chapter will look at attempts being made to change the current system from within.

PROBLEMS WITH STATE SCHOOLING

Is formal schooling really as bad as some seem to think, and are the alternatives any better? Popular songs from the last fifty years have spoken of problems with schooling. For Pink Floyd in 1979 school was 'another brick in the wall' and in the song 'Kodachrome' Paul Simon wrote that high school had taken away his capacity to think. Central to this opposition has been the belief that schooling is weighted too strongly towards the teaching of nationally agreed centralised knowledge. In doing this, it is claimed, education totally neglects the nature and needs of the pupils. But the strongest criticism comes from those who claim that schooling is not producing adults who can think for themselves. On the contrary it is argued schooling is producing people who run with the herd and are fundamentally institutionalised. Opposition of this kind is not new: it has its roots in the European thought and culture of the Enlightenment and in a US tradition which challenged established British ways of doing things.

PROGRESSIVE EDUCATORS: VISIONARIES

In the last 300 years Europe has produced a number of key thinkers who have put their minds to considering education from what might be called a 'progressive' viewpoint. These approaches have their roots deep in European culture. The word 'progressive' was applied in retrospect to some of these thinkers themselves. It originated in the nineteenth century and came to be coupled to change of any kind. In education it meant a change from traditional methods of teaching and learning. Some thinkers and educationalists began to stress the importance of education for its own sake and not merely as a preparation for employment. Education was also seen as an intrinsic right of everyone. Five of the great thinkers in progressive education were the French philosopher Jean-Jacques Rousseau (1712–78), Johann Heinrich Pestalozzi (1746–1827), a Swiss educationalist, his disciple Friedrich Froebel (1782–1852), a German teacher, Rudolph Steiner (1861–1925), an Austrian polymath, and, perhaps the most well known of all, Maria Montessori (1870–1952), an Italian doctor. The last four not only wrote about education; they also worked with children and opened their own schools.

CHILDREN AND CHILDHOOD

Much of educational thinking is underpinned by beliefs about the nature of children and related concepts of childhood. Nineteenth century ideas often grounded in so called Christian beliefs suggested that children were inherently bad: the sons and daughters of Adam and Eve, born in sin, and vigilance was needed to correct their wickedness. Evil was to be beaten out of them: 'Spare the rod and spoil the child'. These beliefs found expression in some nineteenth century education. The infamous school so aptly portrayed in the novel *Jane Eyre* spoke strongly to this point: darkness and dreariness dominate the writing; children pass their days in fear, and resistance is met with cruel punishment.

But this isn't schooling today. These ideas have definitely passed. Haven't they? In some ways they have, but in other ways traces remain. The British still retain an ambiguous approach to young people. On the one hand, children are regarded as innocents: vulnerable, powerless and in need of protection. Paedophiles lurk on every corner. Childhood is extended almost indefinitely, with young people being dependent on their parents for increasing lengths of time. On the other hand children are regarded as potential criminals from whom society must be protected. In England children are regarded as adults at a much earlier age then in most other countries. The age of criminal responsibility in England is ten, whilst in Scandinavian countries it is fifteen. In England children over ten are subject to the full force of the law, whilst in Scandinavian countries they become subject to welfare provision. These attitudes linger on, as the pupils themselves have described, in a schooling system which renders them virtually powerless in terms of deciding their own education. Children still need to be tightly controlled; otherwise they are likely to run riot.

The progressives' approach was different: they were firmly on the side of the child. On the whole, the early progressives believed that children were essentially good. Wordsworth wrote, 'not in utter nakedness, but trailing clouds of glory do we come'. This is a sentiment progressive educators would have agreed on. They argued that, left to their own devices, children have an enormous capacity to develop and learn; on the whole adults only frustrate the process. Rousseau compared pupils with plants: they both need food and water, but can't be *made* to grow. They do it all by themselves. For Pestalozzi the newborn child was like a seed which would grow well if properly treated. He rejected the view that pupils could be moulded and pushed into shape. Childhood is an important stage in its own right and not a preparation for what is to follow. It was a time to connect with nature. These sentiments have re-emerged recently with the increasing awareness that modern-day children may be becoming estranged from the natural world, experiencing it only by way of the media and the world of virtual reality.

BELIEFS ABOUT THE LEARNING PROCESS

It is in the context of the learning process that progressive ideas were most at variance with traditional ideas. For Pestalozzi, writing in the late eighteenth century, education began at birth and the role of the mother was crucial in child development. This was a novel idea and it took Britain a couple of hundred years to grasp the concept. Central to early-years education is the concept of play. In traditional educational thought play is often considered frivolous, not to be taken seriously, a way of passing time until real education can begin. For all progressive educators, however, the idea of play has been really important. Froebel saw children from birth learning through play, and Montessori even went so far as to say that play is the child's work. For Montessori play needed to be well structured but she remained clear that children learn through activity not through teaching by word of mouth. Above all children need to be active in taking responsibility for their own learning. From the progressive educators has come the maxim, start from where the learner is. For learning to be effective it needs to connect to the learner's previous experience. These ideas were often long before their time and they anticipated the work of the constructivist psychologists outlined in Chapter 5.

KEY IDEAS ABOUT THE CURRICULUM

Progressive educators took the view that children need to partici-pate in planning their own curriculum which in turn must be adaptable to the changing needs of the child. The idea of a fixed curriculum was anathema to them. They stressed the importance of going beyond a traditional academic body of knowledge. The cur-riculum needed to employ all the senses. It was insufficient to appeal only to the brain: feelings and sensory experiences were equally valid. For Froebel drama, music and painting were as important as science and mathematics. Above all, he argued, education should not be taught though separate subjects, but should be integrated so that the curriculum reflected the child's experience of the interconnectedness of the world. Steiner believed that, until the age of seven, play, story telling and engagement with nature were crucial.

THE ROLE OF TEACHERS AND ASSESSMENT

Under progressive education the role of the teacher is different from that envisaged in traditional classrooms. For Froebel the teacher needs to be passive and open to the development of the child. Pedagogy as such has held little interest for progressive educators. Montessori believed that teachers should be more humble and should concentrate on their own defects rather than on those of the child. She based much of her work on observations of children at play and concluded that a good teacher has to let the child take the lead in learning. The teacher must follow the child. This is an interesting idea. What exactly does it mean and what implications does it have for early-years education? This is particularly pertinent now that lists, targets and learning outcomes have been engulfing nursery education. Pestalozzi felt such formality was unwarranted. He strongly believed that schooling tended to stunt originality. As far as assessment was concerned, progressive educators regarded it as not being particularly helpful in relation to the learning process. Most assessment, they maintained, does not help children to understand when they had make mistakes, or aid with the correction of errors.

EFFECTS ON MAINSTREAM SCHOOLING: EARLY YEARS AND PRIMARY

Froebel founded the kindergarten (literally 'children's garden') movement which emphasised the importance of early-years education. Focusing on structured play and children's self-direction, it had a significant impact on the provision of nursery and pre-school education in the UK. From the 1920s onwards Montessori's ideas affected pedagogy and how classrooms were organised. Her influence led to the development of high-quality materials for the teaching of maths and science and small-scale movable furniture for early-years classrooms. Progressive ideas also affected primary education in the 1960s, as outlined in Chapter 5. The last twenty years in England have seen many of these ideas abandoned in favour of a formal curriculum, structured in stages, with far more emphasis placed on numeracy and literacy and the more creative subjects being underfunded and marginalised. In Wales, however, the National Curriculum has changed from a more formal early-years approach to one with a stress on play up to the age of seven. In England in 2008, the Early Years Foundation Stage (EYFS) was introduced for pupils aged three to five. This is very different from the National Curriculum. It focuses around broad themes including physical and creative development and encourages active learning. It remains to be seen what effect these developments will have.

SECONDARY SCHOOL EFFECTS

There was no Plowden Report for secondary schools, and they have tended to remain more traditional in approach than primary schools. However progressive methods have had an effect on secondary practice. For example, mixed-ability teaching; the teaching of all children together in the same class was extended into the secondary phase, and a few revolutionary schools taught children in mixed-ability groups all the way up to sixteen. There was a little less whole class teaching and, on occasions, some team teaching. The role of the teacher was also changing with teachers seen more as facilitators and coaches. This was the period in the 1970s and 1980s which took more account of the monitoring of pupils' progress and the development of new ways of assessing it.

PROGRESSIVE EDUCATORS: OTHER VIEWS

The educationalists named above have focused on the needs of individual children. Others have seen education from a different perspective, stressing the benefits of education for the community as a whole. Herein lies a central dilemma of all education: should it be set up to benefit the individual or to promote the general good. Are these two things necessarily in conflict? In a competitive world, and in UK schooling where children compete with each other from an early age, it is difficult to envisage a culture focused more on communal values, but there has always been a movement in education which has emphasised their importance.

Many of these ideas stem from the thinking of the influential US philosopher and educator John Dewey (1859–1952). He did not start out as an educator, but at the beginning of the twentieth century he came to be appalled by what he saw going on in US schools which, he felt, were characterised by strong regimentation and rote learning methods. Above all, he saw formal education as it was practised as being largely irrelevant to everyday life. He thought that there should be a close link between learning and living, and for this a hands-on, problem-solving approach to learning was necessary. This echoes the beliefs underlying north European curricula outlined in Chapter 4.

THE LEARNER AND THE MAP

Dewey represents a milestone in educational thinking because he provides a link between progressive educators and those who felt that this tradition had neglected pedagogy. The progressive tradition provided good insights into how children learn, but they tended to underestimate the potential power of teaching which psychologists such as Vygotsky and Bruner advocated. In conventional education, teaching had largely been concerned with passing on knowledge from one generation to the next. Progressive educators, on the other hand, have wanted to begin with the child's experience. For Dewey both are necessary. In *The Child and the Curriculum* he writes about the two fundamental factors in education: the immature child and the accumulated knowledge of society. Education consists of the interaction between the two, and it fails if it neglects either dimension. The child lives in a personal world bounded by the experience of being in the family. These roots are important and should be acknowledged and respected, but education takes the child out of this world and into a wider context. In a good education, learners experience challenges to what they know and these sometimes clash with family values. Herein lies the probability of difficulties ahead, but also the possibility of exciting growth. Education is not an easy process.

For Dewey the problem with schooling was in the way it was organised. The child experiences the world as a whole and moves easily from one thing to another, while schooling divides the world into separate subjects which do not relate to the child's under-standing. It makes knowledge abstract and removed from childhood experience. The teacher's duty is to get rid of the idea of knowl-edge as something fixed, ready-made and outside the child's experience. A map – a distilled version of what has gone before – should be provided but it must connect to the child's experience and offer the pupil a way forward. Of course, as with all maps, there is a possi-bility of turning off the road and the byways are often more inter-esting. Good teaching must allow such diversion with pupils encouraged to find their own way through. Dewey's emphasis on the role of accumulated knowledge in the education process sets him apart from other progressive educators, but he always main-tained that such knowledge had to be approached with critical thinking and reflection.

EDUCATION FOR DEMOCRACY

It is with education and its importance for democracy that Dewey takes a giant step from other educators. He believed strongly in democracy and in the learning of skills which support its continua-tion. It is easy to forget now that parliamentary democracy was almost lost to the world in the first half of the twentieth century and that at the end of the World War II there remained very few functioning democracies. For Dewey education is the cornerstone of a strong democracy. His ideas rest on the concept of the 'rea-sonable society' where people do not oppress each other and where cultural diversity is respected and tolerated. It is also a society which tries to be equitable and caring. Schools should play an important part in achieving this.

Dewey held the view that state schools were there to serve the public good. They should stay in public hands, actively linked to their local communities, and resist the drive towards teaching only market-related skills. The reasonable society is not created through teaching numeracy and literacy. Debate and compromise, he said, are as important to learn as mathematics and English. Like Durkheim, Dewey maintained that shared habits and routines are the glue which holds society together. School and classroom rules induct pupils into the shared habits of the school community.

Shared understandings get us through the day without too many problems. This presents a difficulty however: the more habitual life is, the less open we are to the change and growth which are essential for progressive societies. Progress comes through collective collaboration in overcoming obstacles. Schools need to teach children the skills to face and overcome difficulties. They need to keep the image of a truly democratic society always within their vision.

More recently others have developed Dewey's ideas. Michael Apple and James Beane writing in *Democratic Schools* agreed that education has a duty to introduce children to democratic ways of thinking. In order for this to happen, democracy must be prevalent at all levels of schooling. There must be democratic school structures such as a school council which genuinely listens to the voices of pupils. Above all, children do not need rote learning or assimilation of key facts; they need an education which helps them understand and demystify the everyday world so that they can see the power structures which underpin it. Apple and Beane argue that progressive education alone is insufficient. Pupils do need to become personally empowered, but they also need to learn more about equity, to understand the experience of marginalised groups and to take small steps towards understanding the world from different points of view.

EDUCATION FOR LIBERATION

Connected to ideas of education for democracy is the work of Paulo Freire. Born in Brazil of middle class parents, he experienced poverty and vowed to fight so that others did not experience similar circumstances. Education was the tool to change the world. But education itself needed to change. He likened traditional education to a banking system where the student was an empty account waiting to be filled. This practice would not produce significant change: there had to be proper dialogue between teacher and student, and that dialogue had to involve a degree of mutual respect and trust. Education is seen as a process rather than a 'commodity' to be consumed. In the course of being educated, the voice of the oppressed would be heard and this is turn would lead to a 'pedagogy of hope'. Paulo Freire has had a profound effect on education in Latin America, but he has also influenced educators across the world. His message has been that education involves action: the educated person is not a passive recipient of knowledge, but someone who actively seeks to change the world. Here education has a strong moral dimension.

DESCHOOLING SOCIETY

The mid twentieth century also produced other thinkers who criticised formal schooling. Central to these was Ivan Illich. In *Deschooling Society* he argued that schools had largely failed to do what they were designed for and, far from encouraging learning, they positively turned students away from education. He thought that formal school undermined pupils' self confidence and their ability to solve problems. He argued that education is seen by society as detached from ordinary life and occurring primarily in schools. This is incorrect: education and learning are everywhere. School had become a place to learn what the system dictated. If you did this properly you were rewarded with certification. It had turned education from a process to a product: a system for addressing the needs of the professionals rather than those of the pupils. In order to rectify this, Illich argued for the creation of 'convivial' institutions where students would have a chance to interact creatively, and where proper account could be taken of their relationship with the natural environment. He also argued for the creation of learning webs to give opportunities and resources for people to learn wherever they were.

DIFFERENT SCHOOLS

Progressive and radical ideas have inspired people to set up their own schools. The Montessori tradition is kept alive by a worldwide system of schools which espouse Montessori's basic beliefs. In Reggio Emilia, a town in northern Italy, Loris Malaguzzi set up a school after World War II which focused on the children deciding on their own curriculum and with their teachers as co-learners. The principles espoused in Reggio Emilia have since spread around the world and their ideas have been adopted in many other schools. Rudolph Steiner inspired a type of schooling which has also spread worldwide and become known as Steiner Waldorf education. It has been particularly successful in dealing with children with learning difficulties. Dewey set up a laboratory school and experimented with strategies for developing democratic citizens. He consciously built connections between school knowledge and aspects of the larger world. An example of this was teaching the local six-year-old sons of farm workers how wheat was distributed from their farms. He achieved this through role-playing and drama. School leavers eventually encountered difficulties, however. They expected to use intelligent action and debate to promote change, but they were undermined by the competitive selfishness they encountered in the wider world. By far the most well known alternative school is Summerhill, a co-educational independent boarding school which was set up in England in 1921 by A. S. Neill.

SUMMERHILL

A. S. Neill had experienced teaching in Scottish schools where, at the time, education was highly regimented and the use of the cane frequent. He despaired at what was happening to children and eventually set up his own school in Suffolk. He said he would have a school where children could 'be themselves'. But what could this mean? He expected few people would disagree with it, but the reality produced massive opposition which has continued until the present day. In his school Neill had no enforced discipline, no specific direction, no moral training and no religious instruction. This flies in the face of all 'common sense' and most of contemporary understanding of what schooling is for.

Neill started with the basic belief that children are fundamentally good and that they will develop best when they make choices for themselves and access education when it is the right time for them. Children, Neill believed, should never be forced to learn. So Summerhill became a school where children chose whether they went to lessons or whether they played all day.

Everyone had an equal vote, pupils and teachers alike, and matters were decided democratically. It was surely a recipe for disaster and indeed as late as 1999 an Ofsted inspection reported that inadequate education was being provided, a root cause of which was non-attendance at lessons. Some children, the report claimed, had not attended maths lessons in two years. Children were not reaching accepted levels of attainment in reading, either.

The school failed its Ofsted inspection. Politicians muttered. It was obvious that such ridiculous ideas would lead to catastrophic results. However, the school and some of its past pupils mounted a counter-campaign. What was the good of measuring a child's reading ability at aged seven when the whole point of the school was to allow children to learn at their own rate? What was important was where pupils ended up, not the route they took to get there. The campaign was successful and Summerhill now has a unique inspection process. It was the first to include children's voices and preceded Ofsted plans to listen to student views. The 2007 inspection report stated that much of what children learn and experience in Summerhill School is outstanding. It particularly highlighted the importance of the democratic running of the school: vindication indeed of a school which set out to give no moral training. Sceptics have pointed to the fact that Summerhill is a fee-paying boarding school which enjoys total parental support and that this places it in a different position from state comprehensives. Nevertheless, it stands as a monument to the possibilities of progressive education and in stark opposition to much traditional schooling.

CHARTER SCHOOLS AND FREE SCHOOLS

In the United States from the mid 1990s onwards, educators, parents and others in the community were given the opportunity to set up their own schools. These became known as 'charter schools'. They were given full responsibility for the purpose, organisation and daily running of the school. Subject to approval, schools could specialise in whatever they wished. Funding is provided by the number and type of pupils, as in all other schools. The charters last for three to five years, when they come up for renewal. A number of surveys have shown that the majority of parents claimed the charter schools were better than their children's previous schools in teaching quality, individual attention, curriculum, discipline, parental involvement and academic achievement. Most teachers said they felt empowered and that teaching was more interesting as a result. However, there were certain detrimental effects for the non-charter schools in the area. These schools reported a loss of pupils, particularly those with supportive parents. Charters did not attract the vulnerable minority or disadvantaged pupils and sometimes had devastating effects on the provision of good education for all, particularly in urban areas. However, there was some evidence that competition from charter schools pushed up standards in nearby neighbourhood schools.

Similar changes have occurred in Sweden. Parents can apply for funding to set up their own school, although in this case they have to teach a core curriculum and basic democratic values. Recent evaluations have suggested that, while education may have been changed as a result, as in America there is no evidence that such schools improve standards overall, and those who benefit are the children who come from well educated backgrounds. These ideas are of interest because they are leading the UK government to assist in the setting up of 'free' schools in England. Under current government plans, parents, teachers and others can apply for funding to set up new schools, and the government has vowed to relax planning laws to allow this to happen. Schooling can take place in a variety of locations, including shops and houses. Advocates have argued that the move will help pupils in disadvantaged areas. It will allow teachers and parents to create good local schools and maybe replace schools which have closed as a result of local authority economies of scale. Critics have argued that free schools will be detrimental to other schools in the area in the same way as they have been in the United States. It remains to be seen what the outcome will be. For parents dissatisfied with the current school system there remains one other option, which is to teach their children themselves.

HOME SCHOOLING

REASONS FOR TEACHING CHILDREN AT HOME

Teaching children at home is legal in all parts of the UK, and the number of children being educated at home is rising. The rules vary between the four constituent parts. It is very difficult to get precise figures, but it is estimated that there are between 20,000 and 80,000. Why do so many people choose to take their children out of school and educate them themselves? The reasons are, of course, varied and they tend to be different from country to country. In the UK some parents choose this option because their children have already had bad experience of school: they may have been bored or frustrated, they may have been falling behind or been bullied. Whatever their experience, these parents see their children as learning little at school and benefiting from a different approach. There are other parents who dislike the current schooling system. Rather like Illich and other progressive thinkers, they feel that schooling is not primarily aimed at educating their children, but rather at serving the needs of the government and education professionals. School is seen as a place where learning is regimented, where little account is taken of the needs of the individual learner and where a good deal of time is given over to written work as opposed to practical experience. It is probably the lack of individual attention and the methods of pedagogy which are the subject of most discontent.

HOME SCHOOLING: THE EXPERIENCE

Home schooling, it is suggested, offers the following experiences. Firstly, it gives the opportunity for a curriculum which is individually tailored to the needs and interests of the child. Many parents start off with a modified version of the National Curriculum but soon adapt it to suit their children. Secondly there are lots of chances for informal learning to flourish. This contrasts with experience in mainstream schooling where the opportunities for informal learning are frequently limited. In school the majority of teaching is formal. Studies in school have shown that there are times when children concentrate less on the task in hand, Monday mornings and Friday afternoons being prime examples. Parents teaching at home can adapt their teaching to suit the requirements of the child. Finally, home schooling offers opportunities to link with the local community in a way which does not occur in more formal schooling, and children are able to learn with a whole range of people of many different ages. Parents frequently see themselves as learners too, and this has had a profound effect on pedagogy.

The objections to school-based education are considerable. Do parents have sufficient expertise to teach their own children? Research suggests that parents find ways around this. Occasionally children will attend formal lessons in subjects that are particularly difficult to teach at home, but on the whole parents cope well with difficult knowledge. As far as pedagogy goes, the flexibility which home schooling allows appears to compensate for any problems, and schools probably have something to learn from parents in this respect. The most common topic raised is the degree to which home-educated children are socially isolated. Once again research suggests that this is not so. Home-educated children in the UK appear on the whole to be self-confident, stable and mature. They benefit from contact with a variety of age groups and are less dependent on their immediate peers, which in some ways makes adolescence a little easier.

There have been other concerns with home education. In a tragic case, Khyra Ishaq starved to death at home due to parental neglect. She was being educated at home. This incident brought calls for home education to be inspected but opposition has come from the home schooling movement itself stating that there were already adequate safeguards in place and it was the failure of other agencies which contributed to Khyra's untimely death; inspection was the very thing which home schooling needed to resist. The Badman Report on home schooling published in June 2009 however reached different conclusions. Graham Badman concluded that provision was mixed, with some parents very committed to the process but others less so. He called for a common national approach to home schooling which balanced the rights of the parents with the rights of the child and took more account of the child's views. His final recommendations included the setting up of a national registration scheme for children educated at home and a revision of legislation to give local authorities more access to a child's home. Perhaps, however, the concern which is the most difficult to answer is the one which raises the question of the degree to which parents are inflicting their own values and world-view on a child, to the exclusion of all others. Home schooling in the United States has raised some of these issues.

HOME SCHOOLING AND RELIGION IN THE UNITED STATES

In the United States it is estimated that over 1.5 million children are 'home-schooled' and the number grew by 15 per cent a year over the decade 2001–10.[1] A large proportion of these are educated at home for religious reasons. Like others who have opted to teach their children away from school, this group of parents cites the inherent horrors of the state education system, but their reasons for doing so are different. They criticise US schools for failing to teach Christianity and for promoting the case for evolutionary theory: Satan is at work. The danger is close to home and sending children to state schools is tantamount to sending them to be educated by the devil. Most of the groups which attack schooling in this way are right-wing evangelical Christian factions. They have a belief that the Bible is the word of God, totally correct and the only route to salvation. Overall they hold fundamentally intolerant views where there is no room for scepticism or uncertainty. Women are deemed subordinate to men and homosexuality and abortion are abhorred. Interestingly, these beliefs include views on politics and economics. They involve faith in free-market economics and a horror of all ideas which might be deemed 'socialist'. Schools, they fear, are inculcating their children with socialist ideas.

It is claimed that children home-schooled in this vein can be taught all subjects from a biblical perspective. Harmful books such as *Harry Potter* and *the Diary of Anne Frank* can be excluded, and parents can control their exposure to negative environments, including secular ideas and peer pressure. Overall, it is claimed, this increases the chances of family unity. A world free of disagreements, conflicts and difficulties is regarded as the ideal. But education at its best is about quite the opposite. It stops children being cocooned and introduces them to a variety of people and ideas which may often be in conflict with home values. It is going through this process which can lead to an individual becoming an educated person. Home-school promoters as a whole have raised important questions about what state schooling is doing at the present time and it is crucial that politicians and educationalist listen to these concerns. But it is also important to recognize some of the tensions that opting out brings. It is not obvious, for example, how home schooling promotes a more equitable, just or tolerant society.

CHANGING TODAY'S SCHOOLS

EDUCATION IN A PARLOUS STATE

This chapter so far has concentrated on criticisms of schooling which have come from outside the state school system. However, there has been a growing tide of dissatisfaction within the system itself. Pupils have spoken loudly of their unhappiness at the way school is organised. Many teachers express similar views. When they came into teaching, they say, they had a vocation and an understanding of the power of education, but now their creativity is dulled; they are endlessly processing children, ticking boxes, grading and sorting students. Head teachers experience similar levels of frustration and educationalists have been vocal in their demands for change.

Richard Gerver, in *Creating Tomorrow's Schools Today*, mounts a searing attack on the current education system. Much of what he says echoes the points already raised in this book, particularly the themes raised by the pupils. The English school system has outlived its purpose and needs fundamentally to change. It was designed to serve the needs of an industrial nation, sorting pupils for jobs in manufacturing industry and has remained largely unchanged for 140 years with only minor tinkering around the edges. This is not only an outmoded and narrow model of education but one which is out of line with changes which have already occurred. A more productive emphasis might be not on fitting pupils for jobs but on developing adaptable, creative individuals who are entrepreneurial, self-confident and with a strong sense of their own strengths and weaknesses.

Gerver presents a dismal picture of schools as inhospitable, prison-like institutions where children are largely expected to be seen and not heard. By this he means not that schools are silent but that the interests and concerns of the pupils are not on the agenda. The focus is always on the teacher and on 'official' versions of knowledge. The pupils are 'herded' through school which they see as a series of hurdles and hoops they are required to negotiate and which have little or no relevance to their real lives. Irrelevant testing schemes undermine learning opportunities so that, by focusing on exams, the so-called high-performing schools are giving pupils the poorest learning experience. Although schools have some power to change this, they are hampered by the need to produce the 'right' kind of results, because teaching pupils how to do well in tests is essential for school survival. Everyone wants change, but education is in the hands of politicians and civil servants. Gerver maintains that politicians have handed schools over to civil service bureaucrats and the result is an unimaginative retrograde system which is out of step with the world we now inhabit.

It would be easy to dismiss Gerver's criticisms as yet another alternative view of schooling, except that he has been at the centre of the system. Writing as a head teacher who radically turned around a failing primary school in England, he is well qualified to comment on the present parlous state of schooling. It is on the question of *learning* that Gerver presents the strongest critique. What children experience in their education is at odds with what is happening in the rest of their lives. Schools, with some notable exceptions, have largely failed to take note of the enormous transformation in the use of technology, changes which have put pupils ahead of the game with teachers trailing behind. These children will have to face the enormous challenges which the world will present and they are already better placed than their elders to cope with what is to come. What schooling now needs to do is to help children manage this technology and, in the process, help them to get a rounded view of the world. Rather than starting with an outdated industrial model curriculum, education needs to start with where the pupils are.

A number of other writers are saying similar things. In *What's the Point of School?* the well known educational psychologist Guy Claxton is equally critical, attacking the concept of 'ability' which underlies current schooling. There may be a different view of intelligence in the early twenty-first century, but little of it has percolated down to schools. Children are still sorted by so-called 'ability' and trained to produce the right kind of results. The curriculum is taught in separate subjects that have changed little in the last 100 years and are out of touch with the world children are experiencing. Like Gerver, Claxton is critical of an assessment system which has been only tinkered with in recent times and which he considers to be fundamentally unfit for purpose.

ACTIVE LEARNING

What these writers and others in similar vein are calling for is no less than a revolution in education based on the idea of children as active learners. We are born to learn and, to one degree or another, learn for the rest of our lives. Babies never give up; they practise and reformulate problems endlessly. To a certain extent this process continues in early years and a little into primary education, but by and large schooling does not nurture and cherish the desire to learn. It is an irony that the place which is supposed to encourage such learning is the environment where it is least likely to happen. All the curriculum documents in the countries of the UK refer to the need for active learners, about developing all pupils, about raising aspirations; but these are words only. They do not, as Claxton points out, translate into action. In reality pupils have no say over what they are learning or the ways in which they are doing it, and yet they have a desire to be active, responsible and to be taken seriously.

Claxton catalogues eight qualities which need to be encouraged in pupils if we want them to be successful learners. Important amongst these are curiosity, courage, willingness to explore and experiment and, above all, imagination. Schooling has to turn itself round so that these attributes are fostered; it is not possible to start with a rigid curriculum. Children need to be guided by their own questions and there own interests. There is no place in schooling for solely transmitting teacher knowledge and ignoring pupils' queries. At the present time pupils are not encouraged to ask questions. Every child learns sooner or later that only certain questions are permissible in class. Teachers say time and time again, 'Ask if you don't understand,' but this relates solely to pupils' inadequacies. I have failed to grasp what is being explained and I have to ask for help. These are not the kinds of questions which further active learning, and pupils understand very quickly that asking questions potentially exposes them to ridicule. Above all learning with others demands courage. Children need resilience and resourcefulness in order to survive; but these attributes, although not encouraged in school, can be taught and should be a high priority. It has always been a hallmark of education in Asian countries, particularly Japan, that children should be taught resilience and persistence and never to give up. In the UK and the United States, however, these virtues are by and large neglected.

COMMUNITY OF LEARNERS

Central to change has been the growing idea of thinking of teaching and learning in a more democratic way. We are all engaged constantly in learning. The growth of lifelong learning is testimony to this. Teachers it is argued no longer control knowledge and they themselves are constantly learning. However, many teachers do not see themselves in this way. As with many other professionals, they feel insecure in any approach which questions their expertise and knowledge. For schools to change, teachers need to change. They need to accept that learning is a joint activity. They need to think of students as people they work with, not people they do things to. This change of direction would bring enormous benefits. It would allow pupils to make a real contribution to the development of understanding. They would become knowledge-makers instead of knowledge-consumers. Rupert Sheldrake, a Cambridge biologist, wrote in *Seven Experiments that could Change the World* about the questions which academic science had ignored, one of which was concerned with the behaviour of pets. Pets he said have interesting and unexplained relationships with their owners. Dogs appear to know when their owners intend to come home, even though the owners do not depart at the intended time. Conventional science, however, is not interested in pet behaviour and therefore has not researched it: gorillas, lions and tigers are much more interesting. Yet research on pets could be done by anyone anywhere. Sheldrake invited schoolchildren to take part in large experiments which would document the behaviour of pets. Knowledge-making could be an important part of the primary school science curriculum.

CHANGES WHICH ARE HAPPENING TODAY

Gerver, with the lively involvement of pupils, teachers, parents and the wider community, actively changed his school into one where the children's imaginations were fired and where children were encouraged to recognise and develop their own unique abilities and interests. This was achieved through a process which returned to the basic question of what the central purpose of their school was and how they could make learning as exciting as going to Disneyland. Pupil empowerment was seen as the key and, with the help of the children, the Grangeton Project was created. This turned the school into a town run by the children themselves. The curriculum was designed around the project with the emphasis on the learning of key skills. The local community responded enthusiastically and came in to help. The project thus utilised current knowledge about learning and brain development. It also included the children themselves understanding how they learnt and what was happening in their own heads. Gerver's account shows how it is possible to transform schools, but it also recognises the difficulties which politicians and civil servants present to would-be challengers.

INTERNATIONAL COMMENT

In March 2010 the OECD produced a PISA report entitled *The High Cost of Low Educational Performance* mentioned in Chapter 2. This gave an analysis of the relative performance of the different educational systems in relation to pupil success or otherwise in the international tests in literacy, numeracy and science. The report linked the level of pupils' cognitive skills to economic performance. It concluded that there are major differences in the education systems of those countries currently doing well in the PISA tests and those not performing as well.

Looking at best practice the reports authors concluded that successful systems such as that of Finland had the following characteristics. They had excellent heads who were rewarded for good leadership rather than bureaucratic accountability. These countries successfully recruited and trained teachers from the top third of graduate distributions, encouraging professional independence, rewarding teachers appropriately. Teachers themselves had a clear understanding of what their job involved. They expected every child to succeed and intervened quickly to ensure it happened. There were also rules and incentives which encouraged the dispersal of talented teachers equitably through the system. These systems contrasted with countries not doing as well; where heads are held accountable for their actions but not professionally empowered; where teachers are from the bottom third of the graduate distribution and are offered training which does not prepare them for the realities of classroom life; where teachers' perceptions of ability preclude all pupils performing well; where seniority and tenure are more important than performance and where the best teachers are operating in the most advantaged communities. The UK falls at the moment into the latter category.

For a country's education system to be successful, the report maintains, investment in education is not enough. There needs to be a paradigm switch. A system needs to move from uniformity to diversity, from bureaucratic accountability to devolved responsibility, from looking beyond provision to the outcomes of such provision. Educational systems have to stop talking equality and start delivering it. Politicians need to stop prescribing what education should be doing and start relying on an informed teaching profession. The report brings together many of the criticisms of the UK system that have been raised in this book. Education does not need more of the same, it says. It needs new ways of thinking, new ways of working and new tools for the job.

UNIVERSITIES FOR THE FUTURE

It is not only in schools that a fundamental rethinking of education needs to take place. Ronald Barnett, in *Higher Education: a Critical Business*, argues that universities have radically to rethink the way they approach teaching and learning. The traditional university was built on the idea of the importance of knowledge, but the current world is 'radically unknowable' and it is into this world that students are graduating. They have to operate effectively in this unknowable world. To this end we need students who have a sense of the world but who can also stand apart from it. Critical thinking, Barnett maintains, is key to this process. Critical thinking is not just about knowledge and reason, it involves critical self-reflection, in the sense that Gerver puts it for children, knowing one's strengths and weaknesses. It also involves action. These ideas are explored further in the final chapter. Critical thinking, critical self-reflection and critical action are all needed to produce the 'durable self'. This has enormous implications for pedagogy. It changes the student and the teacher, and ultimately has an impact on society itself. Everyone – students and tutors alike – needs to see themselves as learners. It involves students being allowed enough space to find things out for themselves. It requires tutors actively to listen to what their students are saying.

CONCLUSION

This chapter has looked at the long history of alternative approaches to education. 'Progressive' educational thinkers have for the past

300 years put the child at the centre of the educational process and suggested modes of education radically different from most found in British schooling today. Many of these ideas are about children learning on their own or with at least the individual child's interests being paramount. But others have focused on the kind of education that can benefit the community as a whole and not just be serving the needs of the individual child. These ideas are fundamentally at odds with education in the UK at the present time with its stress on liberal values where the freedom of the individual is paramount.

Alternative approaches to education have led to the formation of alternative schools. These have ranged from Montessori early-years schools to Summerhill boarding school where different approaches to learning have been tried. They have resulted in an ever-growing number of pupils being home-schooled. International reports such as those from the OECD have suggested that countries doing well in education are operating in a fundamentally different way from those doing less well. People from across the educational spectrum have documented problems with current UK schooling, from an inappropriate curriculum and assessment methods to a top-heavy bureaucratic accountability system. There are widespread calls for education to be revolutionised, more related to the world we actually inhabit and strongly centred on the idea of students and teachers as investigatory and courageous learners.

EDUCATION AND THE WORLD

'It was the best of times, it was the worst of times ... we had everything before us, we had nothing before us,' Charles Dickens wrote in *A Tale of Two Cities*. He could well have been talking about our current predicament. We in the West live in a time of unprecedented opportunity. We are wealthy beyond the dreams of our grandparents. We benefit from huge advances in medical research and improved living standards. Life expectancy of children born today is put at 100 and yet in the UK there are high levels of mental illness and drug and alcohol dependence. We live in a society where there has been an unrelenting increase in the number of people imprisoned and, above all, a growing gap between rich and poor. Report after report indicates that we are not a society which is happy or at ease with itself. Our problems pale into insignificance, however, compared with those in other parts of the world. Much of Africa and parts of Asia and Latin America are extremely poor. Environmental catastrophes present a persistent threat and are spreading to countries which have not previously experienced them. Worst of all, the next generation, no matter where they live, face enormous problems in the form of climate change, peak oil, environmental degradation and international conflicts.

We stand at a point of decision making. What direction do we want the world to take? What future society do we want to live in and what responsibility do we individually have in relation to this? What can be done about the looming problems which face us all? Above all, what role can education play in tackling these seemingly intractable difficulties? The answers to these questions affect our own education and the kind of education we give our children. In the clichéd saying: education is part of the solution or it is part of the problem. To be educated means to know what is happening in the world, to understand why it's occurring and to help find solutions.

STATE OF EDUCATION IN THE WORLD

Primary education is seen as a fundamental human right. It is also seen as essential for economic development and for full participation in the globalised world. In the developed world there is almost unlimited access to education and the vast majority of the population is literate. In the rest of the world the figures are dismal. At the turn of the last century close to a billion people were illiterate and unable to sign their name.[1] In the year 2000 world leaders formulated eight goals for the world which they hoped to reach by 2015. Goal No. 2 is the achievement of universal primary education. The goal is to 'ensure that, by 2015, all children have access to, and complete, primary education that is free, compulsory and of good quality'. Progress to date has been slow. Some 101 million children of primary school age are still not in school.[2] 46 million of these live in sub-Saharan Africa.[3] Much greater effort will be needed if the target is to be reached in sub-Saharan Africa and some of the countries of South East Asia. The reason why countries are not able to provide schooling for young people are mainly to do with poverty, but also with war and natural disasters.

EDUCATION AND POVERTY

The world is a very unequal place, whether measured in terms of income *per capita*, human rights or access to services such as education. Rich capitalist countries account for 16 per cent of the world's population but own 80 per cent of the world's wealth. The poorest countries, which have 57 per cent of the world's population, own 6 per cent of the world's wealth. The World Bank estimated that the poorest 20 per cent consume 1.5 per cent of the world's resources; the richest 10 per cent consume 59 per cent. At least 80 per cent of the world's population lives on less than $10 a day and over one billion people live on less than one dollar a day. Several hundred million people are hungry and a further 350 million people do not receive adequate nutrition.[4] Contrary to opinion people are hungry because they are poor, not because there is insufficient food or land available; they simply do not have enough money to buy food. Debt in the developing world to first World Banks has been steadily rising. These countries cannot pay the interest, let alone the capital. Some debt has been written off, but there are often strings attached. In such circumstances education becomes a luxury rather than a right.

Inequality impacts the most on women and children. The poor tend to be women because they are paid much less than men for the same work, they are less well educated, have fewer legal rights and own less than one per cent of the world's wealth. At least 11 million people in poor countries will die this year from infectious diseases for which there is a cure, half of them children under five. There are two billion children in the world, 1 billion of whom live in poverty. UNICEF has estimated that at least 24,000 children die every day due to poverty.[5]

EDUCATION, WAR AND CONFLICT

Education is often affected by wars and conflicts. Despite the developed world having experienced nearly 66 years of relative peace, the rest of the world has not been so lucky. In 2008 there were 28 armed conflicts in 24 different countries with 39.3 per cent in Africa.[6] Every minute two people are killed in conflict around the world. In South America, Africa, Asia and the Middle East wars are frequent. The United Nations Children's Fund (UNICEF) has estimated that more than a million children died in 2001–10 as a result of war and at least six million have been disabled or seriously injured.[7] They further estimate that there are at least 300,000 child combatants. In many areas children, boys and girls alike, left unprotected, become child soldiers. Many have been forcibly recruited or they have been abducted from their homes. They are trained to fight or serve as sex slaves, frequently brutally intimidated and often forced to commit atrocities. Despite an international agreement to try to eradicate the use of child soldiers the practice persists.

Education does not flourish in war zones. Wars destroy school buildings; students and teachers are killed or have to flee their homes. It was estimated at the end of the twentieth century that less than one per cent of the world's arms bill would need to be spent to provide primary education for all, and yet we cannot manage even this reduction. By any rational yardstick it seems like a world gone mad.

WHY ARE SOME PEOPLE POOR?

A variety of reasons are offered to explain global inequalities. The *pragmatic* – this is the way the world works. The *meritocratic* – the developed countries worked hard, were enterprising and have earned their wealth. They forged the industrial revolution, built empires and now reap the benefits. The *judgemental* – the poor deserve their fate because they are inclined to slothfulness or lack basic ability. The *caricature* – the notion that to be Western and white is to be superior to other people. Perhaps we are not so far from the beliefs of George Gawler, the Governor of South Australia who wrote in 1835 that he was bringing civilization to the aboriginal people (Chapter 3).

Whatever explanations we offer for global inequalities there is always a distancing effect: the issues of poverty are far from home. The media do portray graphic images, but in the end we are mostly able to dissociate ourselves from them. They are not our children, family or friends. We respond by giving something to charity and a small proportion of our national wealth is given in aid. However, this money does not offer a solution to the problem and comes under threat the moment our national circumstances hit harder times. Perhaps we have to dig deeper in our search for understanding. Are these reasons for inequality given above good enough? Are global levels of inequality inevitable? Is it really the fault of the people living in poorer countries that they are so badly off and they have so little access to education? Could there be other explanations more plausible which could lead to a change of understanding and ultimately to action? The history of Africa and its education service offers insights as to how such inequalities came into being and how they are still being perpetuated.

CAPITALISM, COLONIALISM, EXPLOITATION AND INJUSTICE

Africa is the second largest continent in the world, home to around a billion people and made up of 57 countries and territories.[8] It has a long and distinguished past, having been the birthplace of modern humans. The BBC account in 2003, *The Story of Africa*, documented the sophisticated cultures which existed in the West African Kingdoms from the fifth century to the sixteenth. Nevertheless things were about to change drastically in the centuries which followed with the advance of trade, colonialism and capitalism.

Capitalism is an economic system in which the means of production from factories to tools are privately owned and where the goods produced are sold on open markets. People are paid wages for the work they do. The main driver in this system is to provide a profit for the owners and shareholders. The more things which can be sold the better, irrespective of whether there is a need for such products or not. Capitalism began in England but was rapidly exported to the rest of the world. In the beginning it was *anarchic*, in other words not controlled in any way. In order to secure maximum profits nineteenth century factory owners required their employees to work long hours for as low pay as possible. There was mass exploitation of working people. Over time the state intervened to curb the worst excesses of capitalism, for example limiting the hours that children could work. Elsewhere in the international arena capitalism remained exploitative. Western firms sought to increase the amount they produced. Those with money bought and sold goods around the world aided by their various governments which sought to obtain favourable trading terms. In India this famously related to cotton production. Although cotton had originally been woven in India, the British imposed laws which prevented local people from processing it. Many Indians did not own the land on which the cotton was grown and were treated as labourers, not manufacturers. This entrenched the global inequalities which persist to today, with the developed countries often controlling production in a similar fashion. A considerable amount of clothing bought in the West has been produced by people – many of them children – in

Third World countries working long hours in poor conditions. A report published at the end of 2010 by War on Want and Labour Behind the Label alleges that prominent high-street chains get their products from factories in India which are exploiting their workers. The cost of clothes in the UK is held down at the expense of sweatshop labour in India.

What started with trade turned to exploration and then conquest. The 'Scramble for Africa' began in 1884 when a conference in Berlin divided the whole continent between the major European powers. Artificial countries were created whose boundaries took little account of the reality of where people actually belonged. This has contributed to the conflicts which plague the continent. Advanced industrialised nations now supply arms at a price to the various combatants and in some cases the purchase of arms is a condition for the receipt of aid. Little thought or concern was given for the people who lived there, with Africa being seen as a source of raw materials and labour which would service the Western world. Conquest was followed by a long period of colonial rule which eventually ended with independence given to many countries in the 1960s.

The legacy of all this is often unstable democracies or single party states. African leaders are sometimes treated favourably by Western corporations for permitting advantageous trade links. A WikiLeak suggested that an oil company, Shell, had representatives in all the main Ministries of the Nigerian government, the implication being that Shell benefited from the arrangement. Nigeria is very rich in oil, but the majority of its population remain very poor. Children of the better-off elites in African states are often funded through prestigious Western universities and are encouraged to adopt Western values and lifestyles. Corruption is rife. Colonialism left a legacy of debt, with the colonising state often transferring the debts it had incurred to the newly independent state which replaced it.

EDUCATION IN AFRICA

Education in Africa reflects the continent's history. From the beginning there was a history of traditional education. In some areas this still remains and is reflected in the saying attributed to African culture, 'It takes a village to raise a child'. Magnus Bassey in his book *Western Education and Political Domination in Africa* has outlined the key components of such an education. The whole community is responsible for education with it being firmly rooted in everyday life. Parents and elders provide much of the teaching that is often done as in other indigenous societies through play and storytelling. Education seeks to be character-building and often has tests of initiation. It encourages courage and bravery: elements that, critics have complained, Western education systems lack. Nevertheless, there is also considerable gender stereotyping. Traditional education of this kind is in the main participatory and fairly democratic. It was later to be supplanted by the education system which colonisation exported to Africa.

The colonisers brought with them their own systems of education which varied according to their country of origin. The British sought to introduce a curriculum similar to that which followed the 1870 Education Act, namely the three Rs, reading, writing and 'rithmetic, with accompanying Christianity. In early colonial days Cecil Rhodes, the Prime Minister of the Cape Colony, came to epitomise the attitude of the colonisers to their subjects. He saw them as 'barbarians' and expected that the vast majority of them would pass their time in manual labour. Many of the educators were missionaries who sought to convert the local inhabitants to Christianity and there was fierce competition between Catholics and Protestants.

What effect did all this have on education? Colonial education frequently displaced traditional education. In recounting African views of colonial education, Bassey says that they saw the education system imported into the colonies as serving the colonial interests. By and large they felt colonial education separated Africans from their culture, mocked traditional beliefs and enshrined inequality. While recognising the validity of these points the BBC *Story of Africa* emphasised that Christian missionaries also brought literacy and hope for the disadvantaged. The story is complex.

CAPITALISM MANAGED

After World War II there was a consensus that international capitalism should not to be left to its own devices. The international community set up a number of international institutions which were intended to regulate capitalism. Two of these were the

International Monetary Fund (IMF) and the World Bank. The IMF was a public institution funded by international taxpayers. Its main aims were to foster economic growth, to provide temporary financial assistance to countries in difficulties and generally to encourage global financial stability. The World Bank was created to complement the work of the IMF: to help fight poverty and to improve the standard of living for the world's developing countries. Since World War II, these two institutions have worked together and achieved modest success. Many of the sub-Saharan countries began to stabilise and there was some reduction in the levels of poverty.

NEO-LIBERALISM AND AFRICAN COUNTRIES

All this was about to change however. The 1970s produced an oil crisis which sent shocks around the world. Many countries in the West, including the UK, suffered economic difficulties, but the consequences for the newly independent African countries were very serious and they were plunged further into poverty and debt. This was not aided in subsequent years by radical changes in the IMF and the World Bank.

At this point in the story it is time to return to the political philosophies outlined in Chapter 1. Liberalism was once again in the ascendant but it was a form of liberalism radically different from that which had gone before. It was 'neo-liberalism'. Its fundamental tenet is that decisions should be left entirely to the market with the very minimum of state intervention. United States neo-liberal economists had come to believe that economics was a science which had general laws. These could be understood and universally applied in any country in the world, irrespective of its social and cultural background. All that countries needed to succeed was access to free and deregulated markets.

These beliefs were now to be exported to the rest of the world. With the Republicans in power in the United States, a purge occurred in the World Bank and those economists not agreeing with the new orthodoxy resigned. The World Bank and the IMF became intertwined. They combined forces with the US Treasury and reached an agreement about world trade and the free market. It became known as the Washington Consensus. Countries which needed help applied to the IMF and the World Bank supplied loans, but they were linked to IMF conditions: state intervention was to be reduced, privatisation increased and barriers to trade removed. This was often known as 'structural adjustment'. It basically meant cutting public spending.

EFFECTS OF NEO-LIBERAL GLOBALISATION: THE ECONOMY

The results of these policies have often been disastrous in developing countries. Firstly they led to the cutting of essential services such as education, health and welfare. The numbers of children going to school were reduced and invariably it was girls who suffered. This process was accompanied by privatisation, the removal of state ownership and the transfer of assets such as water and electricity to private hands. Privatisation was accompanied by the fast sacking of many workers with no account taken of the social costs. Jobs were lost and not replaced. This process was supposed to attract foreign investment which would help create growth and jobs, but international banks tend to lend first and foremost to international clients who bring in their own staff and expertise. This destroys local initiative. So recipient countries may have wonderful new hotels, international airports and golf courses, but little improvement in the lives of ordinary people – in fact quite the reverse. The speed with which all these things happened has been unprecedented, but privatisation only works successfully if certain conditions exist. Prime amongst these are adequate state–run essential services, not too much corruption and an appropriate legal structure. In most countries needing World Bank help these conditions did not exist. It has led to worldwide criticisms of the IMF, not only from underdeveloped countries but also from prominent Western economists such as Joseph Stiglitz. In his book *Globalization and its Discontents*, he sets out in graphic detail how the IMF has imposed drastic economic policies on developing countries, policies which were designed to serve the financial interests of the West. The IMF, it seems, has failed to achieve the aims it was originally set up for. There are now renewed claims for international capitalism to be restrained.

EFFECTS OF NEO-LIBERAL GLOBALISATION: EDUCATION

Not only have neo–liberal policies affected the funding of education in African countries, they have also affected the type of education on offer. Chapter 1 outlined how education in the UK, driven by neo-liberal policies, has moved from being seen as a public service to being perceived as a marketable commodity. Privatisation and school choice have been the order of the day. These policies, however, have also been exported to countries beyond the UK and the United States. Stephen Ball in his book *The Education Debate* argues that the World Bank has in the last twenty years sought to define the educational policy which should be applied in all countries seeking its financial help. Drawing on the work of Philip Jones, *World Bank Financing of Education*, Ball suggests that loans from the World Bank were accompanied by demands for education to be privatised. Thus the bank brought pressure to bear on African countries to reduce the public money spent on education and to increase the number of private schools where parents are required to pay fees. This has become a virtually unquestioned orthodoxy.

EDUCATION IN ZAMBIA

The historical process outlined above can be seen in any of a number of African countries. One such country is Zambia, a land-locked country in the south of the continent. It was originally inhabited by nomadic tribes, but was finally colonised by the British at the end of the nineteenth century and named Northern Rhodesia. It gained independence from Britain in 1964. Its educational history follows the trajectory of other African countries. It still maintains some of its traditional education but its close ties with the UK mean that it also retains elements of colonial education. English for example is the language used in schools.

After independence free primary education was instigated and school books and other learning materials were provided without payment. However, following the economic downturn of the 1970s, the price of copper, Zambia's chief export, collapsed with a resulting drop in revenue. School materials were charged for and school fees were reintroduced. Following loans from the IMF, 'structural adjustments' were required. This cut the education service further.

Zambia is a country where out of a population of 11.9 million. 6.2 million are under the age of eighteen.[9] Moreover over

1 million of these children are orphans. This is in part due to the devastating effect that HIV and AIDS have had on the country. There is now an urgent need for education. At present education is free from grades 1 to 7 providing a basic education in general subjects, but the country is still a long way from establishing a - reasonable level of secondary education. Schools at primary level are either state-run, private or community establishments. The state schools are very large and have relatively few trained teachers. They often operate two shifts a day. The private schools are frequently run as businesses, with fees depending on the kind of facilities which are provided. Community schools exist in rural areas and also in some high density urban zones and are run by volunteers. Despite many difficulties, the government still has to account to external agencies for the money it spends. Zambia is committed to meeting the 2015 goal of primary education for all. Its progress to date has been good and it is a testimony to both the government and the people that this has been achieved.

IN SUMMARY

To return to the original question of why large parts of the world are in extreme poverty and unable to provide even primary education for their children, the reasons are complex. They are a result of a legacy of conquest and colonisation followed by subjection to a particular economic orthodoxy which has not delivered significant economic improvements. It is not that people of sub-Saharan Africa are lazy or lacking in intelligence. It is rather that they carry a burden that we in the West are largely exempt from. Ha-Joon Chang, writing about capitalism, states that free-market policies of the kind advocated by neo-liberals have rarely worked. Sub-Saharan Africa grew at 1.6 per cent *per capita* terms in the days before neo-liberalism and only 0.2 per cent in the years between 1980 and 2009. The future, however, is not inevitable. Abandonment of neo-liberal policies, employment of better technologies and organizational skills together with improved political institutions could lead to Africa emerging from poverty. Moreover, far from being lazy, the people of sub-Saharan Africa are very entrepreneurial. They have to be to survive.

GLOBAL CHALLENGES

AN UNSUSTAINABLE LIFESTYLE

The cumulative effect of the last 300 years of development has led to a Western lifestyle which is threatening the very planet we live on. It is now not only poorer countries that are suffering. The malaise is spreading to richer countries too and is likely to be rapidly accelerated. We are using up the world's natural resources at an unprecedented rate. Our actions seem to be the main cause of climate change and environmental degradation. If earlier centuries demonstrated an almost unbelievable rapaciousness on the part of those with power and money, the last three decades have seen the desire for wealth and possessions spreading to the majority in industrial societies. We can dissociate ourselves from our communal past, but as workers and consumers we are all involved with the present destruction. Tony Judt's last and seminal work *Ill Fares the Land* is a crushing indictment of the way we live now, where the pursuit of material self-interest has wiped out any other aims for society. We no longer ask such questions as: is it good or just or fair? We are solely interested in what way the subject in question will improve our financial situation and that of our immediate family. This concern with the price of everything has, as Judt states, left us with little understanding of the worth of anything. It corrodes our national life; we have jettisoned our communal aspirations in pursuit of personal gain. It has enormous effects on the kind of society we now live in. It has affected the education we give our children.

GLOBAL WARMING AND CLIMATE CHANGE

For the past thirty years the evidence for man-made global warning has become clearer and clearer. Ever expanding industrial production and the methods used to promote this have led to an enormous increase in the levels of gases such as carbon dioxide, methane and nitrous oxide in the atmosphere. This factor known as the 'greenhouse effect' is causing the polar ice cap to melt, the seas to warm and the climate to change. It is already producing extremes of weather, in some parts of the world drought but in others widespread flooding. The worst effects are felt in poorer countries which have to date contributed by far the least to global warming. In the long term climate change is likely to result in shortages of food, water and energy. This will shape all our futures, but will have a devastating impact on the poorest both at home and abroad. There are those who contest these claims, but this opposition seems to comes largely from think-tanks who support free trade and are funded by the very multi-national energy companies who are likely to suffer the most if curbs to greenhouse gases are put in place. Their objections are not supported by the scientific evidence which all points in the same direction. Climate change seems to be upon us and has largely happened as a result of our actions.

PEAK OIL

The world is closer than ever to running out of oil. Oil discovery reached its apex at the end of the 1960s and has been declining since then. Finding more oil will mean drilling in deeper waters or perhaps extracting oil from tar sands. Whatever, it is likely to be enormously expensive and very dangerous for the natural environment. Demand for oil is on the increase, fuelled not only by the West but also by the expanding economies of India and China. It is central to our very existence. The vast majority of transport is fuelled by oil. Nearly everything we buy in the shops has required the use of oil. We are totally oil-dependent. Energy experts are divided about when the crisis will come, but whichever way it is looked at oil is likely to get ever more expensive. As with climate change, expensive oil impacts disproportionately on the lives of the poor. Moreover, the burning of oil contributes to global warming.

SOLUTIONS

To return to where this chapter started, the world faces a formidable list of problems, most of them interrelated. They may feel overwhelming, but they are not inevitable. The problems are largely the result of human behaviour, and human action can change things. To effect such a fundamental transformation demands an understanding of what is happening in the world and what its causes are. This is where education comes in. All of us need to appreciate the situation we are in and how it has arisen. However, education seems to be lagging behind. *Every Child's Future: Leading the Way*, a piece of work commissioned by the National College for leadership of Schools and Children's Services and written by Jonathon Porritt and others, is a notable exception. They have suggested a number of measures schools can take in preparation for an uncertain future. These include achieving self-sufficiency in energy, bringing the natural world back into the classroom and promoting the importance of diversity, equality and social cohesion. By and large, however, formal schooling seems to be avoiding the fundamental issues. This is part of what has been termed the 'psychology of denial'. The difficulties are seen as so overwhelming and so threatening that pretending they are not happening, or assuming that a technological solution will be found seems the best solution. Education is not helped by the fact that teachers are ill trained to discuss these issues. They are best left alone. Not so with pupils, however. Accounts from children again and again reveal that they are more in tune with what is happening than are adults. Young people are desperate to understand how the world works, to discuss what is happening and to come up with solutions. Research has shown that when children actively engage with the issues their fear recedes.

There are solutions. The international form of capitalism can be regulated, just as European capitalism was regulated in the first half of the twentieth century. There are different forms of capitalism which have flourished and not caused such huge levels of inequality: the collectivist capitalism of Japan, for example, has something to teach the world. Changing our Western lifestyle does not involve returning to the hardships of former times, but it does require a more co-operative and socially aware stance than Britain has managed in the last thirty years. As Tony Judt writes, we have an instinctive understanding and dislike of unfairness, injustice and inequality, but in the public arena we have lost the ability to talk about these issues or to find effective solutions. We have largely left the discussion to politicians, with disastrous results. There is an urgent need, he says, to remedy this.

EDUCATION FOR CHANGE

KNOWING THE FACTS, ENTERING THE DEBATE

Education is crucial in understanding the state the world is now in, the reasons for it and the ways in which problematic trends could be reversed. As Dewey said, pupils need to understand how the world works, including who has power and how it is exercised. Knowing the facts is the first step, but the second is to seek explanations for what is happening, and to find solutions to dilemmas. This is the essence of good education. Ron Barnett writing in *Higher Education: a Critical Business* reflects on a photograph many are familiar with, that of the lone student in 1989 facing the tanks in Tiananmen Square in Beijing. This action he suggests demonstrates a student who is critically aware of the facts, but who is also able to resort to action. Education needs to help pupils be part of the solution. There are many ways in which education is at least making students more aware and some of these are outlined below, but these endeavours still remain at the edges of the curriculum, tangential to the more serious business of demonstrating ability in numeracy and literacy.

LEARNING FROM OTHER CULTURES

We are children of the Enlightenment, brought up with a belief in the power of rational and scientific thought and enjoying the benefits this has brought. Alongside this, however, we have grown up with a view of humans as being different from the rest of creation. The natural world is seen as not being connected to us now as it was to the lives of our ancestors, but rather as something to be managed and exploited for personal and economic gain. Humanity appears to exist apart from the surrounding world and its role is to manipulate nature to serve its own ends. A consideration of other beliefs and values reveals a startlingly different approach to the natural world. Aborigines, for example, have a symbiotic relationship with the land. They do not see themselves as being above nature, but rather as being caretakers and guardians of the earth. Similarly Native Americans traditionally have a sense of kinship with other life forms and feel responsible for living harmoniously with their environment. The education which indigenous peoples have adopted reflects these beliefs. It stresses the need for a long-term perspective which stretches across generations. Thus many changes can only be understood in the light of what has happened in the past and all change must be considered in relation to its impact on the generations to come. All things are interconnected and it is not possible to make sense of the world through the prism of separate subjects. Education needs to be rooted in its local community, but also needs to be constantly changing to fit the times. For most native peoples the power of storytelling, music and drama have been central to young people's understanding of the world around them. Education can teach respect for the world, awe and humility. This way of teaching and these values have been largely overlooked by traditional Western education. Perhaps it is time to re-evaluate them.

SCHOOL LINKS AND UNIVERSITY EXCHANGE VISITS

In recent times a number of schools in the UK have formed links with schools in Africa. This can give pupils the opportunity to get first-hand information about education in another country, but it frequently demands a long-term commitment to the African school. There are also ways of establishing communication via secure on-line learning communities. Similar links have been forged between universities and African schools where university students make visits to the schools in question. Dan Davies and Elaine Lam in *The Role of First-hand Experience in the Development Education of University Students* investigated whether such visits challenged the stereotypical images that British students often have of life in sub-Saharan Africa. Despite citing benefits for the students concerned, the authors reported that many of the ethnocentric stereotypes remained and were even sometimes strengthened. They concluded that visits alone are insufficient. To make sense of what is happening, students need a much stronger understanding of issues such as colonialism, globalisation, the politics of international aid and inequality in world trade

UNDERSTANDING GLOBAL INTERCONNECTIVITY

We no longer live in a world of individual states corralled from the rest of humanity. We have in some senses become globalised. This is a term which is much disputed, but basically is the process by which interactions between humans occur across global distances with increasing intensity, speed and regularity. Marshal McLuhan in 1962 coined the phrase 'the global village'. He suggested the instantaneous reception of communications would change nations irrevocably. It was likely to produce the homogenization of cultures worldwide. To a degree this has happened. We know snippets of what is going on in other parts of the world. We all eat pizza and a large portion of the world speaks Mandarin Chinese, Spanish or English. We wear clothes and trainers made in China, use computers made in Taiwan, know that the McDonald's in Barcelona is essentially the same as the ones in Boston, Berlin or Mumbai. But globalisation also concerns us: we want to preserve our national identity and cultural heritage whilst at the same time benefiting from more communication. Globalisation has not brought greater understanding of people living in different parts of the world. In the main, we do not see the ways in which we are all connected or the implications of this for issues of equality and justice.

Educationalists have for the last three decades been urging the need for the inclusion of a global dimension in the school curriculum. The aim of such education is to develop the knowledge, attitudes and skills needed for living responsibly in a multicultural society and an interdependent world. Learning about these issues, they have argued, can help young people understand the impact of present policies on the lives of future generations. Covering issues such as wealth and poverty, rights and responsibilities, conflict and co-operation and environmental concerns can help students consider the best ways to tackle the interrelated global challenges. It also has the potential to make people more independent thinkers, more socially aware and more tolerant. It can motivate learners to want to change things for the better. Such concerns are now increasingly recognised as central to curriculum planning; the 2009 QCA document *Cross-curriculum Dimensions: a Planning Guide* stresses the need for a global dimension in the curriculum. Here are some of the key questions that students and teachers need to ask. How can I enjoy a good quality of life without transferring problems to people in other parts of the world? How can I become an active global citizen and help look after the planet for future generations? These cover the key concepts of interdependence, local–global connections and sustainable futures which global educators have long argued for.

FUTURES EDUCATION

In recent years there has been a growth in the recognition of the need to have a futures perspective in education. David Hicks in *Lessons for the Future: The Missing Dimension in Education* has done pioneering work in bringing to the notice of teachers and educators the futures dimension. He has argued that it is vitally important that pupils understand the relationship between past, present and future. Whilst past and present activities are dealt with to some extent in schools, the future remains mostly off limits. Drawing on academic future studies, Hicks suggests that pupils should be encouraged to think critically about the future for a number of key reasons. Firstly it helps with clarifying values, allowing children to explore what kind of society they would like to live in, and what their own place would be in this. While not being able to predict future change, it does allow young people to anticipate change, enabling them to deal more effectively with uncertainty. Through critical thinking, creative imagination and decision-making processes pupils begin to move from being mere passive receptors of whatever happens to being active and conscious creators of tomorrow's world.

One of the most potent tools which can be used in schools and universities both with teachers and students is the envisioning of probable and preferable futures. In considering probable futures students can be encouraged to imagine what their own futures are likely to be and the future world they are likely to inhabit. These views can be contrasted with the futures they would prefer to have. How are these different from the ones they predict as most likely to happen? For many students and their teachers doing this exercise the gulf is enormous. What they want to happen and what is likely to happen are often poles apart. Of course, the next question has to be, why is this so and how can the gap between the two be reduced? Thinking through the answers to this dilemma and discussing it with peers begins to create a shift in awareness. It is potentially empowering because it allows the individuals concerned to look in detail at the reasons for the disparity. These may be related to low aspirations, but they may also be related to the existence of genuine barriers to progress and change for the better. These kinds of activity link with those suggested by Gerver and Claxton outlined in Chapter 6.

LIVING SUSTAINABLY

In the last decade there has been growing awareness not only of the recognition of global issues, but also of how the local and global connect. One of the key factors in relation to this is living in a sustainable manner. In 2007 the Department for Education and Skills (DfES) produced a *National Framework for Sustainable Schools* which calls for schools to look at how they organise their work so that they have a less negative impact on the world around them. This needs to be demonstrated not only in what children are learning, but also in how the schools themselves are functioning as sustainable organisations. Education for sustainability draws on the previous work done in global and development education, but also draws on environmental education. It brings together some of the key thinking from these fields. Environment and future develop-ment are now totally connected and the welfare of people and planet depend on how these connections are played out. Global warming, peak oil and the limits to growth will ensure that tomorrow will be very different from today. All schools, therefore, need to help with creating a more sustainable future. Guiding principles for sustainable schools cited by the Department for Children, Schools and Families (DCSF) in *Planning a Sustainable School* involve the commitment to care for oneself, others and the environment. This includes teaching and learning about personal health and welfare, but also that consideration be given to others, whether they are living near or at a distance, already here or yet to come. It must take due account of the local and the global environment.

LIVING HOPEFULLY

Finally, but perhaps most crucially in education for change, is the necessity for giving students at school or university access to hope and optimism. The need to understand the problems the world confronts, and to face probably difficult times ahead can result in desperation or resignation, but there are numerous sources of hope which people have drawn upon in times of trouble. These can be found in many different ways. People draw strength, for example, from the beauty of the natural world and the wonder it inspires, from the memory of collective struggles successfully won, and in the stories of ordinary individuals who have triumphed against all the odds. Indeed myths and stories through the ages, whether they are spiritual, political or social, have offered inspiration and hope. Perhaps above all and faced with doom and gloom a sense of humour is paramount. Having fun is probably a key component in the struggle for constructive change, but having courage is also an immeasurable asset. TED global, an annual meeting of thinkers at the forefront of their professions concluded in 2010 that what we need now are good ideas, and lots of them. There are grounds for optimism in this: we belong to a group of higher primates which has an enormous capacity for collective intelligence. When one idea meets another the results are often extraordinary. We may not be able to achieve this level alone, but together there is no end to the possibilities to be achieved. The big question for education is how it can be applied to these ends. The challenge for all of us is how we can release the power for intelligent constructive action and how we can utilise the talents of all students in pursuit of these ends.

EDUCATION: CONCLUDING THOUGHTS

The process of writing this book has thrown up a number of issues which need further consideration. The first of these is the need to think much more about what the purposes of education are. Formal state education was indeed formed to serve the needs of the newly industrialised economy, but the world has changed. We face an uncertain future. Perhaps this form of education has indeed outlived its usefulness and the focus of education in the future needs to change. If so decisions have to be made about the direction education should take. Related to this is the ever pressing question of how good learning takes place and where it can best be fostered. Have schools got it right and if not what changes need to ensue? The relationship between education and democracy is often neglected, but in the UK it is a question which urgently needs addressing. How can education help to produce citizens who are fully informed and prepared to play an active role in promoting democracy? Above all how we can balance the needs of the individual with the needs of society as a whole? The UK has long prized individual freedoms, but these appear to have come at the price of inequality. In the last thirty years belief in the value of the market and individual choice has led to the neglect of the wider society and social democratic values. Does this matter, and if it does, how can a better balance be achieved?

EDUCATION: THE CHALLENGE

At the heart of education there has to be a vision of the world we want to inhabit. It is this vision which seems lacking from present-day British schooling. From progressive educators to people working within the current school system there is a clarion call for change. Education has been about making a difference in the world. People drawn to teaching have always known this, but the possibility of teachers alone effecting such change is now remote. There are so many questions to answer. Do we as a society have the will to radically rethink what we are offering our children and young people? Do we have the foresight to go beyond the narrow world views that current schooling offers? Can we trust the young to contribute to the debate? Can we give them real responsibilities in relation to the future? Education has enormous potential. It can give us new insights, change minds and actively involve us in creating a different world. Do we have the will to take up the challenge?

NOTES

1 Education and schooling

1 DCSF (2009) *Education and Training Statistics for the UK*, ref. ID: VO1/ 2009, Crown copyright.
2 Ibid.
3 R. Pring and G. Walford (1997) *Affirming the Comprehensive Ideal*, London: Falmer Press.
4 Sutton Trust (2010) *The Educational Backgrounds of Members of Parliament in 2010*, copyright, all rights reserved, Sutton Trust.
5 Pring and Walford, *Affirming the Comprehensive Ideal*.
6 HEFCE (2010) *Trends in Young Participation in Higher Education: Core Results for England*, Bristol: HEFCE, p. 62.

2 What are the purposes of schooling?

1 House of Commons Information Office (2010) *Women in the House of Commons*, Factsheet M4, Members Series, London: HMSO.
2 Centre for Advancement of Women in Politics (2010) *Women Members in the UK Judiciary*, Belfast: University of Belfast.

3 Who are the students?

1 DCSF (2009) *Education and Training Statistics for the UK*, ref. ID: VO1/ 2009, Crown copyright.
2 DCSF (2009) *Schools, Pupils and their Characteristics*, London: DCSF.
3 DCSF, *Education and Training Statistics for the UK*.
4 DCSF, *Schools, Pupils and their Characteristics*.

5 HEFCE (2010) *Trends in Young Participation in Higher Education: Core Results for England*, Bristol: HEFCE.
6 HEFCE (2010) *Student Ethnicity: Profile and Progression of Entrants to Full-time, First Degree Study*, Bristol: HEFCE.
7 University of Oxford (2010) *Undergraduate Admissions Statistics, 2009 Entry*.
8 DfE (2009/10) National Curriculum Assessments at Key Stages 2 and 3 in England, 2009/10.
9 DCSF, *Schools, Pupils and their Characteristics*.
10 HEFCE, *Student Ethnicity*.
11 Helen Nugent, 'Black people "less intelligent," scientist claims', *Sunday Times*, 17 October 2007.
12 Jonathan Bradshaw (2005) *A Review of Comparative Evidence on Child Poverty*, York: Joseph Rowntree Foundation.

4 What are we teaching students and why?

1 Quoted in Russell Stannard, 'We can't know everything', *Observer*, 12 September 2010.

5 Teaching, learning and assessment

1 DCSF (2009) *Education and Training Statistics for the UK*, ref. ID: VO1/2009, Crown copyright.

6 Alternative views of education

1 National Center for Educational Statistics (2010) *Home Schooling*, Washington DC: NCES.

7 Education and the world

1 UNICEF global databases, 2008, and UNESCO Institute for Statistics Data Centre, 2008.
2 Ibid.
3 UNICEF (2009) *The State of the World's Children*, special edition *Celebrating Twenty Years of the Convention on the Rights of the Child*, New York: UNICEF.
4 Global Issues, http://www.globalissues.org, *Poverty Facts and Stats*, accessed 10 December 2010.
5 Ibid.
6 'Armed Conflicts Report, 2009', *Ploughshares Monitor*, Vol. 30, No. 2, Waterloo, Ont.: Project Ploughshares.
7 UNICEF, www.unicef.org/protection/index_armedconflict, accessed 10 December 2010.
8 United Nations Statistics Division, New York: DESA.
9 UNICEF, www.unicef.org/infobycountry/zambia.htlm, accessed 12 December 2010.

FURTHER READING

TOP TEN

These are ten books which are each an interesting read. They cover a wide spectrum of content and vary in their level of level of difficulty but all are rewarding. Apple, M. W. (2001) *Educating the 'Right' Way*, London: Routledge Falmer. This is a book about US education which charts how a shift to the right in that country has had a strong effect on school, curriculum and pedagogy. It is important because much of American policy often finds its way to the UK. Ball, S. (2008) *The Education Debate*, Bristol: Policy Press. This gives an account of education policy in the UK. It focuses in a lively way on government policy interventions in the last twenty years and shows the impact they have had on education. Burke, C. and Grosvenor, I. (2003) *The School I'd Like*, London: Routledge Falmer. This is a fascinating read which draws on pupils' views of schooling in the 1960s and at the turn of the century. Through pupils' eyes we get an insight which is interesting, enlightening and at times shocking. Chang, H. (2010) *Twenty-three Things They Don't Tell You about Capitalism*, London: Allen Lane. This is a provocative book which takes current beliefs about the economic world we live in and shatters them. It is particularly pertinent in relation to education. It turns what we know on its head. Gerver, R. (2010)

Creating Tomorrow's Schools Today, London and New York: Continuum. A good example of how one head teacher turned a failing school round. It's full of practical examples but it also questions current beliefs about the nature and purpose of schooling. Holt, J. (1991) *How Children Learn*, Harmondsworth: Penguin. Written in the 1960s, this is now a classic. It is fundamentally a book about children. It suggests that teachers should trust their pupils' innate ability to learn and stand back from teaching them too much. Neil, A. S. (1998) *Summerhill: a new View of Childhood*, New York: St Martin's Press. Neill gives his own account of the school he started, the radical philosophy which underpins it and his beliefs about parenthood and child rearing. It questions what most people in education take for granted. Orr, D. (2004) *Earth in Mind*, Washington, DC: Island Press. David Orr lays bare the relationship between economics, ecology and education. He suggests that we need a drastic shift in teaching and learning in order to cope with impeding crisis. The book is full of practical suggestions. Robinson, J. (2009) *Bluestockings: the Remarkable Story of the First Women to Fight for an Education*. London: Penguin Viking. It is easy to forget that until very recent times women were denied access to education. This brings the story home and reminds us in a very readable way what women owe to those who fought on their behalf. Wilkinson, R. and Pickett, K. (2009) *The Spirit Level: why More Equal Societies almost Always do Better*, London: Allen Lane Penguin. A controversial book that demonstrates that countries which are more equal almost always have healthier people with longer life expectancies, and better educational outcomes. The UK is not doing well in this regard.

HELPFUL TEXTBOOKS AND COMPILATIONS

Arthur, J. and Davies, I. (eds) (2010) *The Routledge Education Studies Textbook*, London and New York: Routledge.

Bartlett, S. and Burton, D. (2007) *Introduction to Education Studies*, London: Sage Publications.

Hicks, D. and Holden, C. (eds) (2007) *Teaching the Global Dimension: Key Principles and Effective Practice*, London: Routledge.

Matheson, D. (2008) *An Introduction to the Study of Education*, London: David Fulton.

McKenzie, J. (2001) *Changing Education: a Sociology of Education since 1944*, Harlow: Pearson.

Meighan, R. and Harber, C. (2007) *A Sociology of Educating*, London: Continuum.

Ward, S. (ed.) (2008) *A Student's Guide to Education Studies*, second edition, London and New York: Routledge.

Ward, S. and Eden, C. (2009) *Key Issues in Education Policy*, London: Sage Publications.

REFERENCES

Alexander, R. (ed.) (2009) *Children, Their World, Their Education: Final Report and Recommendations of the Cambridge Primary Review*, London: Routledge

Apple, M. (2002) *Educating the 'Right' Way*, New York and London: Routledge Falmer

Apple, M. and Beane, J. (1995) *Democratic Schools*, Alexandria, VA: Association for Supervision and Curriculum Development

Badman, G. (2009) *Review of Elective Home Education in England*, London: Stationery Office

Ball, S. J. (2003) *Class Strategies and the Education Market*, London and New York: Routledge Falmer

Ball, S. J. (2008) *The Education Debate*, Bristol: Policy Press

Barnett, R. (1997) *Higher Education: A Critical Business*, Buckingham: SRHE and Open University Press

Bassey, M. O. (1999) *Western Education and Political Domination in Africa: A Study in Critical and Dialogical Pedagogy*, Burnham, PA: Greenwood Press

BBC (2003) *The Story of Africa*, www.bbc/worldservice /specials/1624_ story_of_africa

Bennett, N. (1976) *Teaching Style and Pupil Progress*, London: Open Books

Berger, P. and Luckmann, T. (1967) *The Social Construction of Reality*, London: Penguin

Bernstein, B. (1977) *Class, Codes and Control* (3 vols), London: Routledge

Blanden, J., Gregg, P. and Machin, S. (2005) *Intergenerational Mobility in Europe and North America*, London: Centre for Economic Performance. Copyright, all rights reserved, Sutton Trust

Blatchford, P., Bassett, P., Brown, P., Martin, C., Russell, A. and Webster, R. (2009) *The Deployment and Impact of Support Staff in Schools*, Research Report DCSF-RR 154, London: Institute of Education, University of London

Bowles, S. and Gintis, H. (1976) *Schooling in Capitalist America: Educational Reform and the Contradictions of Economic Life*, London: Routledge & Kegan Paul

Bourdieu, P. (1984) *Distinction: A Social Critique of the Judgement of Taste*, London: Routledge

Burke, C. and Grosvenor, I. (2003) *The School I'd Like*, London: Routledge Falmer

Carrington, B., Tymms, P. and Merrell, C. (2008) 'Role models, school improvement and the "gender gap": do men bring out the best in boys and women the best in girls?' *British Educational Research Journal*, Vol. 34, No. 3, pp. 315–17

Chang, H. (2010) *Twenty-three Things They Don't Tell You about Capitalism*, London: Allen Lane

Claxton, G. (2008) *What's the Point of School?* Oxford: Oneworld

Davies, D. and Lam, E. (2010) 'The role of first-hand experience in the development education of university students', *International Journal of Development Education and Global Learning*, Vol. 2, No. 2, pp. 35–52

Dawson, R. E., Prewitt, K. and Dawson, K. (1977) *Political Socialization*, Boston, MA: Little Brown

DCSF (2008) *Planning a Sustainable School: Driving School Improvement through Sustainable Development*, London: Department for Children, Schools and Families

Dewey, J. (1902) *The Child and the Curriculum*, Chicago: University of Chicago Press

DfES (2007) *National Framework for Sustainable Schools*, London: DfES

Douglas, J. W. B. (1964) *The Home and the School*, London: MacGibbon & Kee

Durkheim, E. (1956) *Education and Schooling*, Glencoe, IL: Free Press

Freire, P. (1972) *Pedagogy of the Oppressed*, London: Penguin

Friedman, M. (1962) *Capitalism and Freedom*, Chicago: University of Chicago Press

Galton, M. and Simon, B. (1980) *Progress and Performance in the Primary School (Oracle)*, London: Routledge

Garcia, E. E. (2001) *Hispanic Education in the United States*, Lanham, MD: Rowman & Littlefield

Gerver, R. (2010) *Creating Tomorrow's Schools Today*, London and New York: Continuum

Goffman, I (1968) *Asylums: Essays on the Social Situation of Mental Patients and other Inmates*, London: Penguin Books

Harber, C. (1991) 'International contexts for political education', *Education Review*, Vol. 43, No. 3, pp. 245–56

Hicks, D. E. (2006) *Lessons for the Future: The Missing Dimension in Education*, Crewe: Trafford Publishing

Hirst, P. H. (1975) *Knowledge and the Curriculum*, London: Routledge and Kegan Paul

HMI (1978) *Primary Education in England*, London: HMSO

HMI (1980) *A View of the Curriculum*, London: HMSO

HMI (1992) *Teaching and Learning in Japanese Elementary Schools*, London: HMSO

Illich, I. (1976) *De-schooling Society*, London: Penguin Books

Jackson, P. W. (1991) *Life in Classrooms*, new edition, New York: Teachers' College Press

Jones, P.W. (1992) *World Bank Financing of Education: Lending, Learning and Development*, second edition, London: Routledge

Judt, T. (2010) *Ill Fares the Land* London: Allen Lane Penguin

Kerr, J. (2006) *The Tiger who came to Tea*, London: HarperCollins

Macpherson, W. (1999) *The Stephen Lawrence Inquiry*, London: HMSO

Maxwell, J. (1983) 'Is Mathematics Education Politically Neutral?' M.Ed. dissertation, University of Birmingham

National Conference on Infant Mortality (1908) *Infant Mortality*, Westminster: P. S. King

Norwood, C. (1943) *Curriculum and Examinations in Secondary School*, London: HMSO

OECD (2009) *PISA 2009 Results*, Paris: OECD

OECD (2010) *The High Cost of Low Educational Performance*, Paris: OECD

Orr, D. (2004) *Earth in Mind*, Washington, DC: Island Press

Plowden Report (1967) *Children and their Primary Schools*, London: HMSO

Porritt, J., Hopkins, D., Birney, A. and Reed, J. (2009) *Every Child's Future: Leading the Way*, Nottingham: National College for Leadership of Schools and Children's Services

QCDA (2009) *Cross-curriculum Dimensions: A Planning Guide for Schools*, London: Qualifications and Curriculum Authority

Rist, R. C. (1970) 'Student social class and teacher expectations', *Harvard Educational Review*, Vol. 40, No. 3, pp. 411–51

(Robbins) Committee on Higher Education (1963) *The Report*, London: HMSO

Robinson, J. (2009) *Bluestockings: the Remarkable Story of the First Women to Fight for an Education*, London: Penguin Viking

Rosenthal, R. and Jacobson, L. (1968) *Pygmalion in the Classroom*, New York: Holt Rinehart & Winston

Rudduck, J. and McIntyre, D. (2007) *Improving Learning through Consulting Pupils*, Abingdon: Routledge

Sennett, R. (1999) *The Corrosion of Character: The Personal Consequences of Work in the New Capitalism*, New York and London: W. W. Norton

Sheldrake, R. (1995) *Seven Experiments that could Change the World*, New York: Riverhead Books

Stiglitz, J. (2002) *Globalization and its Discontents*, London: Allen Lane Penguin

Swann Report (1985) *Education for All*, London: HMSO

Walum, L. R. (1977) *The Dynamics of Sex and Gender: A Sociological Perspective*, Chicago: Rand McNally

War on Want and Labour Behind the Label (2010) *Taking Liberties: the Story behind the UK High Street*, London: War on Want; Bristol: Labour Behind the Label

Warnock Report (1978) *Special Educational Needs*, London: HMSO

Wiki, L. (2005) *Politics Remains a Man's World*, London: Institute for Public Policy Research

Wilkinson, R. and Pickett, K. (2009) *The Spirit Level: Why More Equal Societies almost always Do Better*, London: Allen Lane Penguin

Willard, W. W. (1965) *The Sociology of Teaching*, London: John Wiley

Willis, P. (1978) *Learning to Labour: How Working Class Kids get Working Class Jobs*, Farnham: Ashgate

Wood, E. K. and Millichamp, P. (2000) 'Changing the learning ethos in school', *Journal of In-service Education*, Vol. 26, No. 3, pp. 499–515

Young, M. D. (1970) *The Rise of the Meritocracy*, London: Penguin

INDEX